Sharing
Digital Photos
FOR DUMMIES®
PORTABLE EDITION

**by Julie Adair King,
Mark Justice Hinton,
and Barbara Obermeier**

WILEY

Wiley Publishing, Inc.

Sharing Digital Photos For Dummies®, Portable Edition

Published by
Wiley Publishing, Inc.
111 River Street
Hoboken, NJ 07030-5774
www.wiley.com

Copyright © 2010 by Wiley Publishing, Inc., Indianapolis, Indiana

Published by Wiley Publishing, Inc., Indianapolis, Indiana

Published simultaneously in Canada

Trademarks: Wiley, the Wiley Publishing logo, For Dummies, the Dummies Man logo, A Reference for the Rest of Us!, The Dummies Way, Dummies Daily, The Fun and Easy Way, Dummies.com, Making Everything Easier, and related trade dress are trademarks or registered trademarks of John Wiley & Sons, Inc. and/or its affiliates in the United States and other countries, and may not be used without written permission. All other trademarks are the property of their respective owners. Wiley Publishing, Inc. is not associated with any product or vendor mentioned in this book.

For general information on our other products and services, please contact our Customer Care Department within the U.S. at 877-762-2974, outside the U.S. at 317-572-3993, or fax 317-572-4002.

For technical support, please visit www.wiley.com/techsupport.

Wiley also publishes its books in a variety of electronic formats. Some content that appears in print may not be available in electronic books.

Pocket Edition ISBN: 978-0-470-59146-8

Manufactured in the United States of America

10 9 8 7 6 5 4 3 2 1

Table of Contents

● ●

Publisher's Acknowledgments

We're proud of this book; please send us your comments at
`http://dummies.custhelp.com`. For other comments,
please contact our Customer Care Department within the U.S. at
877-762-2974, outside the U.S. at 317-572-3993, or fax 317-572-4002.

Some of the people who helped bring this book to market include
the following:

Acquisitions, Editorial

Senior Project Editor:
Mark Enochs

Executive Editor: Steve Hayes

Editorial Manager:
Leah Cameron

Composition Services

Senior Project Coordinator:
Kristie Rees

Layout and Graphics:
Ronald Terry, Erin Zeltner

Proofreader: Susan Hobbs

Publishing and Editorial for Technology Dummies

Richard Swadley, Vice President and Executive Group Publisher

Andy Cummings, Vice President and Publisher

Mary Bednarek, Executive Acquisitions Director

Mary C. Corder, Editorial Director

Publishing for Consumer Dummies

Diane Graves Steele, Vice President and Publisher

Composition Services

Debbie Stailey, Director of Composition Services

Introduction

● ●

*W*elcome to *Sharing Digital Photos For Dummies,* Portable Edition. It's official: Digital photography is no longer considered a fleeting fad or solely a game for techno-types. Today, everyone from preteens to great-grandmothers is recording their memories with digital cameras, abandoning their old film models to the attic, the basement, or worse.

This growing enthusiasm for digital photography is for good reason, too. The features and quality packed into today's digital cameras are nothing short of astounding. Tiny, fit-in-your pocket cameras are now capable of producing images that, in some cases, surpass those of professional models from five or six years ago — and at prices that were unheard of in years past. Digital SLR models, which accept interchangeable lenses, are now remarkably inexpensive, too, making the step up to semi-pro features much more accessible to enthusiastic shutterbugs.

For many people, though, figuring out how to use all the features offered by today's cameras, let alone how to download, organize, and share digital photos, is an intimidating proposition. *Sharing Digital Photos For Dummies,* Portable Edition answers all your questions about sharing photos in easy-to-understand language, with a dash of humor thrown in to make things more enjoyable. This book spells out everything you need to know to make the most of sharing your digital photos with friends and family.

What's in This Book?

Sharing Digital Photos For Dummies, Portable Edition covers all aspects of sharing your photos. Whether you want to learn how to post your photos online (with a service like Flickr) or email your photos to friends, this book will help you get started. There are also chapters on printing and scanning your photos as well as how to set up a digital frame.

Conventions Used in This Book

When you need to choose a command from a program menu, you see the menu name, an arrow, and then the command name. For example, if you need to choose the Print command from the File menu, you see this instruction: Choose File⇨Print.

Sometimes, you can choose a command more quickly by pressing keys on your keyboard than by clicking through menus. These keyboard shortcuts are presented like so: Press Ctrl+A. This simply means press the Ctrl key and the A key at the same time, and then let up on both keys. When shortcuts differ depending on whether you're a Windows or Mac user, the PC shortcut appears first, followed by the Mac shortcut.

Icons Used in This Book

Like other books in the *For Dummies* series, this book uses icons to flag especially important information. Here's a quick guide to the icons used in *Sharing Digital Photos For Dummies,* Portable Edition:

This icon represents information that you should commit to memory. Doing so can make your life easier and less stressful.

 The Tip icon points you to shortcuts that help you avoid doing more work than necessary. This icon also highlights ideas for better ways to share your pictures.

 When you see this icon, pay attention — danger is on the horizon. Read the text next to a Warning icon to keep yourself out of trouble and to find out how to fix things if you leaped before you looked

Where to Go from Here

That's all you need to know to get started. Whenever you hit a snag as you try to share your photos with friends and family, just look up the topic in the Contents at a Glance and turn to the coverage you're looking for. *For Dummies* books are designed so that you can dip in anywhere that looks interesting and get the information you need. This is a reference book so don't feel like you have to read an entire chapter (or even an entire section for that matter). You won't miss anything by skipping around. So find what interests you and jump on in!

Chapter 1

Sending, Posting, and Copying Photos to Disk

* *

In This Chapter

▶ Getting ready to share your photos

▶ E-mailing photos

▶ Posting photos to the Web

▶ Creating CDs and DVDs of your photos

* *

*T*he more you develop your digital photography skills and the more photos you take, the more likely you'll want to share your photos with family, friends, and associates. You can easily attach a photo to an e-mail message and send that to one person or a group.

To share a lot of your photos, or to share them with a number of different people, you might consider using an online photo-sharing service or even a *blog* (short for weblog), a personal Web site that is simple to create and maintain. And besides e-mailing your photos, you may want to create slide shows that you can burn to a CD, DVD, or flash drive. This chapter tells you how to get started with all of these photo-sharing methods.

Preparing to Share Photos

You can enjoy sharing photos with your friends and family in various ways after you get your photos in the right location (on your computer) and identified (organized and labeled) so you can find them. To get your digital images onto your computer where they're available for sharing through e-mail or online postings, you must transfer them from your camera.

Photo organizing software enables you to do just that — move photos from your camera to a computer. And as the name implies, such software helps you organize your photos so you can find specific photos when you want to. With photo organizing software, you can easily arrange your photos into folders or by name, date taken, location taken, and so forth. With the right photo organizing software, you can also add titles, comments, and even ratings to your photos.

Choosing a photo organizer program

Photo organizing software helps you manage your photos. With an organizer, you can find, copy, move, rename, and delete photos. Most organizers also include some photo editing tools, so that you can rotate, crop, and fix photo problems.

The following organizers are free or included with certain cameras or computers:

> ✔ **Your camera's software:** Some cameras include a disc with software for viewing, organizing, and editing your photos. If a disc came with your camera, you may want to install the included software. If you decide to use a different program, you do not need to install the disc that came with your camera or you can uninstall the included software if you switch to another program.

✔ **Windows Live Photo Gallery:** This software is available for free as a download from Microsoft for Windows XP, Windows Vista, and Windows 7 users. If you have Windows Vista, you may already have Windows Photo Gallery, which is the predecessor to Live Photo Gallery. Live Photo Gallery has a few improvements over the older program, including more editing options. See Figure 1-1.

Figure 1-1: Windows Live Photo Gallery is available online for free.

If you already have Windows Photo Gallery (the one without Live it its name), you can follow many of the steps in this book. If you run into something you can't do, then you can download and install the Live version.

✔ **Picasa:** This program is free from Google. Picasa is very popular and a good choice as a photo organizer. Picasa may be slightly harder to use than Photo Gallery because of the way Picasa presents its many options. See Figure 1-2. Picasa does have some interesting features beyond Photo Gallery's, including an easy way to add text directly to photos.

Figure 1-2: Picasa has many photo viewing and editing options.

Google released a Mac version of Picasa just as this book went to press, making Picasa the only free photo organizer I know of that works on both Windows and Mac. See www.picasa.com for information and the download.

✔ **iPhoto:** This program is included on Macs as part of the iLife suite of programs. iPhoto is not available for Windows users. See Figure 1-3.

Of course, there are other choices for photo organizers. A very popular program is Adobe Photoshop Elements, which costs money, unlike the programs I've already listed. Elements is a powerful photo editor with its own organizer features.

Figure 1-3: iPhoto is for Mac users only.

 You can use any organizer and photo editor or even more than one. They all have some functions in common, including those covered in this book.

Transferring photos from your camera to your computer

If you have a camera that comes with a cable, you can use it to connect your camera to your computer. See Figure 1-4 for the typical USB connection. Your computer will have USB connections in the back (thin rectangular sockets), but you may also find connections on the front of the computer tower or on your monitor or keyboard.

Figure 1-4: The computer end of the USB connection.

 If you have to use the USB sockets in the back, buy a USB extension cable or a small box called a *hub*, which provides additional USB connections. Plug the extension cable or hub into the back of your computer. Then you can more easily plug devices into the extension or hub, which you place for easy access.

1. **Plug one end of the cable into the computer with the computer on, and with the camera off, plug the other end of the cable into the camera.**

   Look for the socket on the side or bottom of the camera, as shown in Figure 1-5. The socket might be covered with a small plastic or metal piece that slides or pops open.

2. **Turn on the camera, and the computer detects the camera automatically.**

   The first time you do this, you may see the AutoPlay dialog box in Figure 1-6. If so, do one of the following:

   • To match the steps in the book, choose Import Pictures and Videos Using Windows

Live Photo Gallery. Don't choose Import
Pictures Using Windows because that would
use a different program.

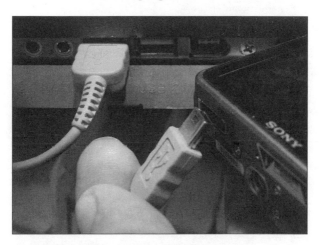

Figure 1-5: Find your camera's cable connection.

- If you choose another organizer, such as
  Picasa, you have to adapt the steps in the
  book.

- If you do not want to use any organizer,
  choose Open folder to view files using
  Windows Explorer (this is not shown in
  Figure 1-6 — scroll to bottom of the dialog
  box) to copy photos from the camera to your
  computer.

If you choose Photo Gallery in AutoPlay, the
Import Photos and Videos dialog box appears.

3. **Choose Import All New Items Now (as shown in
   Figure 1-7) and, in the related text box, type the
   text you want to use in naming folders and
   photos.**

Figure 1-6: Choose an option in the AutoPlay dialog box.

Figure 1-7: Name your imports here.

You can use the More Options link to confirm or
change the Import Settings.

4. **Click the Import button to begin copying your
   photos.**

   You'll briefly see each photo as it is copied. See
   Figure 1-8. Check the Erase After Importing
   option if you want to remove the photos from
   your camera's memory card after they have been
   copied successfully to your computer.

(Otherwise, you have to delete those photos on your own.) You see the erasing process after the importing completes.

Figure 1-0: Photos being copied show up briefly.

5. **After the copying is done, Photo Gallery starts up, and you see your newly copied photos on your screen.**

   If you don't see your photos, click Pictures on the left side of the screen.

Copying photos from a memory card to your computer

Instead of connecting your camera to the computer, you can use a memory card reader to copy photos from your camera to the computer. A *memory card reader* is a small device — either built in to the computer or separate — into which you directly insert memory cards. (There is no advantage in using a reader if you also have a cable for your camera.)

1. **Locate your memory card reader. If the memory card reader is a separate device, plug it into a USB port.**

   If you haven't used the memory card reader before, Windows may install a device driver the first time you use it.

2. **With your camera off, remove its memory card after opening the cover in the bottom or side of the camera.**

   Some cards are held in place by a small latch you move out of the way. If the card doesn't pop out, gently push in against the card. Let go and the card should pop out partway. Do not pull or pry the card out if it does not pop out when you push and release. Gently pull the card out the rest of the way, noting how it was inserted, so you can put it back later.

3. **Gently push the memory card into the appropriate slot in the memory card reader.**

   Some readers have multiple slots, so you may have to guess which slot to use and the correct way to insert it. Keep your thumb on the card's label with metal contacts away from your hand. Push the card into a likely slot until it clicks and stays in place when you let go of it. If it doesn't go after applying slight pressure, take the card out, rotate it, and put it back in.

4. **If the computer detects the card, Windows should run the AutoPlay function automatically. Choose an import option:**

   • Import pictures and videos using Windows Live Photo Gallery.

   • Open Folder to View Files.

   Either Photo Gallery or Explorer may open automatically without giving you a choice.

5. **Follow the prompts of your organizer or Windows Explorer to copy the photos from the memory card.**

6. **When you're finished copying, return the memory card to your camera.**

If you are using Windows Explorer, it opens showing
the contents of your camera's memory card, as in
Figure 1-9. You can copy any folders, but you may
want to open folders until you see photos (start with
a folder named DCIM). Then you can copy the photos
without the folders. The photos you copy this way
will have the filenames that the camera gives them.

Figure 1-9: See what's on your camera's memory card.

Adding descriptions to your photos

You can use the Info pane in Windows Live Photo
Gallery — or the relevant view in your photo
organizer — to add or change various details that
describe your photos. Figure 1-10 shows the Windows
Live Photo Gallery interface. If the Info pane does not
appear on the right side of your screen, click the Info
menu item at the top of the screen to bring it up. Click
on one of your photos to select it. The information
you can change appears in black.

- ✔ **Caption:** Click on Add Caption and type in a caption for your photo. You can use upper- and
  lowercase letters, numbers, and spaces in the
  title. One reason to title photos is that you can
  later search for photos based on text in the title.

- ✔ **Filename:** Click on the current filename if you
  want to change it. The filename can be used to
  search for and sort photos. If you have multiple
  photos selected when you enter a new name,

Photo Gallery adds a number to distinguish them, such as *my photo, my photo (1), my photo (2).*

Figure 1-10: Photo Gallery shows you photo details.

✔ **Date Taken:** You can change the date and time the photo was taken. This is an odd capability. (By the way, if you're up to something nefarious, don't count on fooling legal authorities with this feature.)

✔ **Rating:** Rate your photos with one, two, three, four, or five stars (the best). You can use a star rating to find photos. After you have rated some photos with stars, you can display just photos with that star rating or higher.

✔ **Author:** The author is actually the photographer. Enter your name here.

The remaining information in the Info pane appears in gray and cannot be changed here. However, information about the file and the camera settings may be useful to you, as shown in Figure 1-11. Consider this information:

- **Size:** How big the photograph is in bytes. Larger files take up more disk space and take longer to send with e-mail.

- **Dimensions:** This is the width and height of the photo in pixels. Dimensions up to 800 wide x 600 high are good for e-mail. Dimensions up to 1024 x 768 are good for Web pages. Larger dimensions are better for printing.

- **Camera:** Your camera records its model number with each photo.

- **Exposure:** This is the shutter speed used by the camera for this photo, whether set automatically or manually. You can learn more about the effects of camera settings by observing this information on the photos you take.

- **Aperture:** This is the size of the lens opening when the photo was taken. These are fractions, so f/2 (or F2 on your camera's LCD) is wider (more open) than f/16, which admits less light.

- **Focal length:** This number identifies the amount of zoom in use at the time the picture was taken. For the camera in this example, 5mm is the wide angle setting and 15mm is the maximum zoom. (This camera has a 3X zoom, because 15mm is 5mm times 3.)

- **ISO** (from the French name of the International Organization for Standardization): This number describes the light sensitivity of the image sensor, which records the photo. The greater this number, the more sensitive the sensor is to light, but the lower the quality of the resulting image. Standard ISO is 100, and your camera automatically adjusts ISO as needed.

Figure 1-11: Photo and camera information.

Adding tags to your photos

Tags are categories you assign to your photos, such as the subject or location of the photo. If you took photos of city sights and wildlife while on vacation in Canada, you might tag all the photos as Canada, the city photos as Jasper or Banff, and the wildlife photos as moose or sasquatch. With these tags, you can easily see just the photos of moose or all the photos from Canada, among other variations. In a sense, tags are like separate photo albums or collections of photos, except that one photo can be in more than one collection.

Because any photo can have many tags and any tag can be assigned to many photos, tags provide a very useful way to organize your photos. With tags, you can quickly display a specific set of photos regardless of where on the disk they are stored. Indeed, photos in different folders can be brought together using tags. In effect, if you use tags, it doesn't matter where your photos are stored.

One way to add tags to photos is to do it as you import them. During the import process, you see a dialog box like the one in Figure 1-12.

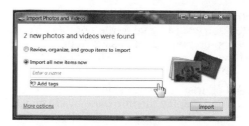

Figure 1-12: Add tags while when you import photos.

Below the box where you enter text that will be added to the folder name and filenames, you see another box for tags. As you enter more than one tag, use semicolons to separate them. If you tag other photos from other occasions with any of the tags you enter here, you can quickly display all similarly tagged photos by clicking on that tag under Descriptive Tags in the Navigation pane. Then click the tag you want under Tags for photos with that tag.

If you see a photo under more than one tag, you do not have more than one copy of that photo. A single photo can be under many different tags. Don't delete a photo just because it doesn't belong under a tag: You'll be deleting the only copy you have. Instead, just remove that tag from that photo. (I tell you how to do that coming up.)

After your photos have been imported into Photo Gallery, you can tag them anytime. There are several different methods for tagging in Photo Gallery:

> ✔ You can drag and drop photos onto the tag you want to give to the photo. Select multiple photos using the small check box in the upper-left corner of each photo. Then click and hold down the left mouse button as you drag the

photos to the left. Hover the mouse pointer over the tag you want to give to the photo(s). You'll see a pop-up message that says Apply (the tag you hover over). Release the left mouse button to finish the process.

✔ Instead of drag and drop, select one or more photos and display the Info pane by clicking Info at the top of the screen. Click Add Descriptive Tags in the Info pane and type a tag. As you type, Photo Gallery displays tags that match what you are typing, if any do. You can type in brand-new tags this way or select an existing tag from the list that pops up.

You can remove a tag from one or more selected photos. In the Info pane on the right, hover over the tag you want to remove. A small X appears to the far right of that tag. Click the X to remove that tag from the selected photo(s). This does not delete the tag, which may still be applied to other photos.

 Under Descriptive Tags in the Navigation pane on the left, you can click the right mouse button over a tag to rename or delete it. If you rename a tag — say, from friend to friends — that tag changes in every photo it was assigned to. If you delete a tag, you remove it from every photo that was assigned that tag, but you don't delete those photos or other tags. You cannot undo deleting a tag from the Navigation pane.

You can even put tags under other tags. Follow these steps:

1. **Under Descriptive Tags, click Create a New Tag and type your tag name.**

   In this example, the tag name is Southwest.

2. **Click Create a New Tag again and type a related, subordinate tag name.**

This example uses the name *New Mexico*.

3. **Click and hold the left mouse button as you drag the second, subordinate tag over the first tag and release the button to drop one tag on the other.**

   In this example, New Mexico is under Southwest. You can repeat the process for Arizona, as shown in Figure 1-13. Tag one or more photos with New Mexico and one or more different photos with Arizona.

4. **To quickly see all photos related to all subordinate tags, you simply click the top-level tag.**

   To see all your photos from New Mexico and Arizona at once, click on Southwest.

Figure 1-13: Create levels of descriptive tags.

The photos themselves may be from different photo sessions and stored in different folders on the computer. Tags bring them together.

Finally, Photo Gallery has a separate category of tags called People tags. With a photo of people selected, you may see a link that says 1 Person Found or 2 People Found (or more). Click that link to view the photo. Photo Gallery draws a box around each face in the photo. (Sometimes, Photo Gallery does not recognize faces that are at an odd angle or are shadowed by hats or sunglasses. You can draw a box yourself around any faces that Photo Gallery misses.)

Click the box or the Identify link on the right and select a name or type in a new name. Figure 1-14 shows the single photo view with the face box selected. If the selected face is your own, click That's Me!

Figure 1-14: Tag; you're it!

Using People tags is similar to using the other descriptive tags. You can click on a person's name to see all photos containing that person, no matter when or where the photo was taken or where the photo is stored.

Sending Photos by E-Mail

As you've probably figured out by now, digital photography allows for instant gratification: point, shoot, and view your photo all in a moment. With the widespread use of e-mail, sending a photo to someone else is nearly as instantaneous.

E-mail programs abound. Some are online or Web-based, such as America OnLine (AOL) and Google Mail (Gmail). Other programs store everything on your hard drive, such as Microsoft Outlook or Mozilla Thunderbird.

Most e-mail programs offer one or two options for including images in an e-mail:

- ✔ Some programs let you insert or paste your photograph directly into the message and control placement and the wrapping of text around that photo.

- ✔ All e-mail programs let you attach a photo as a file, in which case the message recipient either sees your photo just below the text of the message or has to open the attachment separately. Which way the photo appears depends on the recipient's e-mail program.

The single most important issue in e-mailing photographs is the size of the photo. The larger the file size, the longer it takes to upload, transmit, and download the photo. The larger the image in pixels (width and height), the likelier the recipient is to have some problems viewing the photo. Potential problems vary with the recipient's e-mail program and his or her familiarity with viewing photographs.

The easiest thing for you is to insert or attach your photo as is. For the recipient, that photo may be no problem at all. However, be aware of two common problems for recipients of large photos:

✔ **Display issues:** For inserted images, screen size and resolution differences between your computer and the recipient's may affect the appearance of the inserted image. How much space the image occupies and how the text wraps around the image depends on image size (which you choose) and screen size (which is beyond your control).

In the worst case, the recipient sees a small corner of the image and has to scroll horizontally and vertically to pan over the image or take other steps to view the photo.

Figure 1-15 shows an inserted image that is just too big. This photo of a sunflower should be resized or attached to the e-mail instead of inserted.

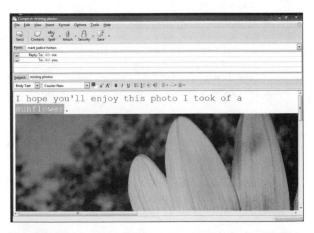

Figure 1-15: Images inserted into an e-mail message should be small enough to be seen completely in the message area.

✔ **Dealing with attachments:** If you attach images rather than insert them, your recipient may avoid resolution problems. Some e-mail programs, however, also show attached images within the message itself, just as if they had been inserted, with the same potential for problems as noted in the preceding bullet.

An image that does come through to the recipient as an attachment can pose other problems. The recipient has to save the attached file, find it, and open it successfully. This process can be difficult for users with little e-mail experience or little experience in dealing with attachments.

 If you want the recipient to see the full-sized version of a large original — especially if the recipient is planning to print the photo — attach the photo, don't insert it. But for easy on-screen–only viewing, reduce the image size (800 x 600 pixels works for most) and insert the photo into the message. Consider cropping the photo to emphasize the subject and reduce the size.

Inserting a photo into an e-mail

After you have edited a photo to the size you want and are ready to insert it into your e-mail, follow these steps:

1. **Open your e-mail program. Type as much of the message as you want. (You can add more later.)**

2. **Place the cursor where you want the image.**

3. **Look for a menu item such as Insert⇨Image or a button showing a frame, camera, or tree. Choose the menu command or click the button.**

4. **Browse to the location of the photo and select that file.**

   Alternatively, you may be able to drag and drop the photo from its location into your message. (Dragging and dropping it may serve to attach the file rather than insert it into the message.)

 You may be able to drag the image within the message and wrap text to the left or right of the image. Look for wrapping options under Properties for the selected image (right-click the mouse).

Attaching a photo file to an e-mail

When you want to attach an image, or any file, to an e-mail, follow these steps:

1. **Open your e-mail program.**

2. **Compose your message (or do so after these steps).**

3. **Look for the word Attach (or Attach Files), a pull-down File menu with an Attach option, or a paperclip button that indicates attaching.**

   The action you have to take here to attach a file depends on your e-mail program.

4. **When the Browse box appears, browse to where the photo is stored on your computer and select the file.**

   The name of the file you are attaching should appear above or below the message area.

 Your photo organizer or photo editor may offer an e-mail option. That option may also allow you to specify the size of the e-mail attachment. If this option is available, the organizer resizes a copy of the original photo before sending it.

The videos you create with your digital camera are large files. Rather than attach them to e-mail, upload them to a video service and send the link to that site in an e-mail. (See the following section, "Posting Photos Online," to find out more about using online photo services.)

Posting Photos Online

Putting photos on the Web has several advantages over e-mailing photos. You can put more photos on the Web than you can reasonably e-mail to anyone. You can tag your photos for arrangement into virtual albums. And more people can discover your photos on the Web and comment on them.

Many services host online photos, and most offer free account options as well as fee-based accounts that give you additional features or allow you to post a greater number of images.

Some online services are integrated with photo organizers. For example, Google's Picasa photo organizer has online capability, as does Microsoft's Windows Live Photo Gallery. A few photo organizers can be customized to work with more than one photo host.

Hosted photos usually allow for a title, description, and tags to categorize a photo. Some services can read this information from the photo's metadata; all allow manual changes to the text associated with a photo.

The more photos you want to share, the better the choice of a photo host may be for you. Blogs are equally good for posting text and photos online and are discussed in the upcoming section, "Adding photos to a blog."

Uploading to a photo-sharing site

Here are just a few popular photo-sharing sites you
may want to consider, although a number of others
are available (try entering *photo sharing services* into
a search engine):

- ✔ www.flickr.com (Yahoo)
- ✔ www.picasa.com (Google)
- ✔ get.live.com (Microsoft)

Web photo hosts require you to create an account,
but you can usually set one up quickly and easily for
free. During account setup, you will choose a user-
name that may become part of the Web address you
give to people to see your photos, such as www.
flickr.com/photos/*mjhinton*.

All photo hosts provide the means to upload one
photo at a time. Many have methods for uploading
more photos simultaneously using a photo organizer
or separate uploading tool. During uploading, you
may be able to limit the viewing of photos to friends
or family, although most photos are freely visible to
anyone on the Web. Just think, digital content from
e-mail and the Web may haunt you decades from now.

Most photo services can optionally resize your
photos for best file size on the Web. Figure 1-16
shows a screen from the upload process in Flickr.

You can also upload the videos you take with
your digital camera. Flickr accepts short videos
(90 seconds or less). YouTube (Google) is a very
popular video host. After posting a video on
YouTube, you can send your friends a link to
that video or even embed the video for people
to see on a blog or other Web page.

Figure 1-16: Upload photos singly or use a separate process to upload batches of photos.

Adding photos to a blog

A blog (from the term *weblog*) is different from other Web sites in that the content is generally updated frequently and the blog entries appear in reverse chronological order — most recent entries at the top, older as you read down.

Blogs can serve almost any purpose. They can be as personal as a diary, or they can help people with a common interest share information or stay in touch. Blogs are even used by corporations to communicate with customers.

Blogs are natural places to post photographs, with or without descriptive text. The photo services in the previous section could be thought of as specialty blogs, displaying your most recently uploaded photos first.

Your photo organizer or your Web photo host may provide tools for uploading (or linking) your photos to blog entries.

Here are three blogging services you might consider using:

- ✔ www.wordpress.com is a popular blog host with photo capabilities.
- ✔ www.blogger.com is owned by Google, as is Picasa, which can add photos to your blog.
- ✔ www.live.com is owned by Microsoft. Live. com hosts both photos and blogs, with sharing between them. Windows Live Photo Gallery can upload to the photo service or the blog service (as well as to Flickr or Picasa).

Figure 1-17 shows the image upload dialog box from Blogger. You can browse your computer or specify a Web address for an existing photo (for example, an image on Flickr). The layout options control wrapping of text around the image (if it is small enough). Image size roughly specifies a size — the uploaded copy of the original will be resized automatically.

Flickr has a Blog This function that works with each of the blogging services just listed. You upload your photo to Flickr and use the Blog This button to send that photo to your blog account with another service, where the photo becomes part of a new blog entry.

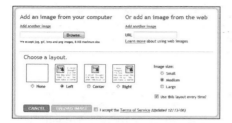

Figure 1-17: Upload images directly to your blog account.

Following basic Web rules

If you want your Web site to be one that people love to visit, take care when adding photos (and other graphics, for that matter). Too many images or images that are too big quickly turn off viewers, especially viewers with slow dialup connections. Every second that people have to wait for a picture to download brings them a second closer to giving up and moving on from your site.

To make sure that you attract, not irritate, visitors to your Web site, keep these nuggets of information in mind:

✔ **For business Web sites, make sure that every image you add is *necessary*.** Don't junk up your page with lots of pretty pictures that do nothing to convey the message of your Web page — in other words, images that are pure decoration. These kinds of images waste the viewer's time and cause people to click away from your site in frustration.

✔ **If you use a picture as a hyperlink, also provide a text-based link.** (A *hyperlink,* in case you're new to the Internet, is a graphic or bit of text that you click to travel to another Web page.) This suggestion applies whether you use a single image as a link or combine several images into a multi-link graphic, or *image map.* Why the need for both image and text links? Because many people with slow Internet connections set their browsers so that images do not automatically download. Images appear as tiny icons that the viewer can click to display the entire image. This setup reduces the time required for a Web page to load. But without those text links, people can't navigate your site unless they take the time to load each image.

✔ **Save Web-bound photos in the JPEG file format.** This format produces the best-looking on-screen pictures, and all Web browsers can display JPEG files. PNG (pronounced *ping*) is a less-common image standard on the Web, and JPEG 2000 is a newer version of JPEG that has yet to be adopted and put into use.

✔ **Don't save photos in the GIF or TIFF format.** If you're familiar with Web design, you may be wondering about using the GIF format for your online photos. GIF, which stands for *G*raphics *I*nterchange *F*ormat, is a great format for small graphics, such as logos. But it's not good for photos because a GIF image can contain only 256 colors. As a result, photos can turn splotchy when saved to this format, as illustrated by Figure 1-18. And the TIFF format, although great for printing, produces files that are too large for Web use and can't be displayed in Web browsers.

People argue about whether to say *jiff,* as in *jiffy,* or *gif,* with a hard *g.* We go with *jiff* because our research turned up evidence that the creators of the format intended that pronunciation. But it doesn't matter how you say GIF as long as you remember not to use it for your Web photos.

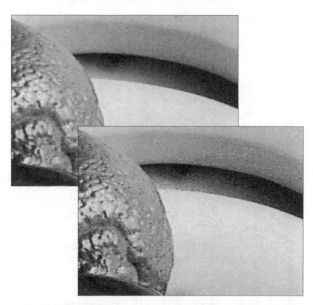

Figure 1-18: For better-looking Web photos, use the JPEG file format (top). GIF images can contain only 256 colors, which can leave photos looking splotchy (bottom).

✔ **Understand how pixel count affects display size.** To accommodate the widest range of viewers, size your images with respect to a screen display of 800 x 600 pixels. Don't forget that the Web browser or e-mail program needs part of the available screen space. For e-mail pictures, a maximum image width of 450 pixels and a maximum height of 400 pixels are good guidelines.

Note that with this low pixel count, people can't make a decent print from your pictures. Consider using a photo-sharing Web site instead of e-mail if you want people to have the option of printing your photos.

✔ **File size determines how long it takes other people to download your pictures.** It also determines how long you sit and wait for pictures to make it from your computer to the Web. If you need to send someone high-resolution images for printing, you can either mail the images on a CD or use a specialized Web application designed to upload, store, and distribute large files, such as the Online File Folder from GoDaddy.com.

✔ **Pixel count, not ppi, determines file size.** File size is determined by the total number of pixels in the image, not the output resolution (pixels per inch, or ppi). The file size of an 800 x 600-pixel image is the same at 72 ppi as it is at 300 ppi.

✔ **Increasing the amount of JPEG compression is another way to reduce file size.** The next section explains this option.

✔ **If you want to control the use of your photos, think twice about posting them online.** Remember, anyone who visits your page can download, save, edit, print, and distribute your image — without your knowledge or approval unless you have a way of protecting your images online (provided by some online photo gallery services, such as Printroom.com). To prevent unauthorized use of your pictures, you may want to investigate digital watermarking and copyright protection services. To start learning about such products, visit the Web site of one of the leading providers, Digimarc (www.digimarc.com). The Web site operated by the organization Professional Photographers of America (www.ppa.com) provides good background information on copyright issues in general. Many image-editing programs also let you add a watermark to your photos (such as your name or a logo) to protect them.

Would you like that picture all at once, or bit by bit?

When you save a picture in the JPEG format inside a photo editor, you usually encounter an option that enables you to specify whether you want to create a *progressive* image. This feature determines how the picture loads on a Web page.

With a progressive JPEG, a faint representation of your image appears as soon as the initial image data makes its way through the viewer's modem. As more and more image data is received, the picture details are filled in bit by bit. With *nonprogressive* images, no part of your image appears until all image data is received.

Progressive images create the *perception* that the image is being loaded faster because the viewer has something to look at sooner. This type of photo also enables Web-site visitors to decide more quickly whether the image is of interest to them and, if not, to move on before the image download is complete.

However, progressive images take longer to download fully, and some Web browsers don't handle them well. In addition, progressive JPEGs require more RAM (system memory) to view. For these reasons, most Web design experts recommend that you don't use progressive images on your Web pages.

If you decide to go with the GIF format instead of JPEG, by the way, you encounter an option called *interlacing,* which has the same result as a progressive JPEG. For reasons illustrated in this chapter (refer to Figure 1-18), you shouldn't really use GIF for photos, but if you do, don't create interlaced files.

JPEG: The photographer's friend

JPEG (*jay-peg*) is the standard format used by digital cameras to store picture files. If you don't need to resize your JPEG originals, you can share them via e-mail or post them on a Web page immediately. All Web browsers and e-mail programs can display JPEG photos.

Chances are, though, that your originals are too large for on-screen use, which means that you need to dump some pixels, following the instructions earlier in this chapter. After you take that step — or do any other photo editing — you must resave the file in the JPEG format before sharing it online.

When you save a file in the JPEG format, the picture undergoes *lossy compression.* This feature creates smaller file sizes by dumping some image data, which can reduce picture quality. The greater the level of compression, the worse the picture appears. In most programs, you can specify the amount of compression you want when you save your JPEG file.

The following steps show you how to use the Photoshop Elements Save for Web utility to save your picture in the JPEG format. Using this feature enables you to see how much damage your picture will suffer at various levels of JPEG compression. If you're using another image editor, check the Help system for the exact commands to use to save to JPEG. The available JPEG options should be much the same as described here, although you may or may not be able to preview the compression effects on your picture.

1. **Choose File⇨Save for Web to display the Save for Web dialog box, shown in Figure 1-19.**

    The preview on the left side of the dialog box shows your original picture; the right-side preview shows how your photo will look when saved at the current settings.

2. **Select JPEG from the Format drop-down list, labeled in Figure 1-19.**

   After you select JPEG, you see the other save options shown in the figure.

3. **Set the compression amount by using the Quality controls labeled in the figure.**

   A higher Quality setting results in less compression and a larger file.

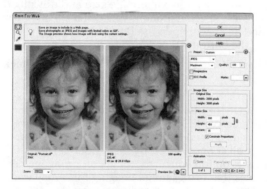

Figure 1-19: The Quality settings determine how much compression is applied.

The Quality drop-down list offers five general settings:

- Maximum (provides the best picture quality/ least compression)
- Very High
- High

- Medium

- Low (provides the least quality/most compression)

If you want to get a little more specific, use the Quality slider on the right. You can specify any Quality value from 0 to 100, with 0 giving you the lowest image quality (maximum compression) and 100 the best image quality (least compression).

When you adjust either control, the right preview in the dialog box updates to show you the effect on your photo. Beneath the preview, the program displays the approximate file size and download time at a specific modem speed. To specify the modem speed, open the Preview menu by clicking the button labeled in Figure 1-19.

4. **Deselect the Progressive and ICC Profile check boxes.**

   If you see a check mark in a box, click the box to remove the check mark and turn off the option. Progressive JPEG files aren't a good idea (for reasons discussed in the "Would you like that picture all at once, or bit by bit?" sidebar). The ICC Profile option concerns some color management issues that professional imaging folks may want to investigate, but us ordinary mortals don't need to worry about. In addition, the option adds to the file size.

5. **If your picture contains transparent areas, choose a Matte color.**

   This feature comes into play only if you're using some advanced Elements features (namely, a multi-layered image that has transparent areas on the bottom layer). So you can ignore it if that doesn't fit your scenario.

6. **Click OK.**

   The Save for Web dialog box disappears, and the Save Optimized As dialog box comes to life. This dialog box works like any file-saving dialog box. Just give your picture a filename and specify where you want to store the file. The correct file format is already selected for you.

   If the original picture file was captured in the JPEG format, be sure to give your Web version a different name, or you overwrite the original image.

7. **Click Save or press Enter.**

   The program saves the JPEG copy of your picture. Your original photo remains open and on-screen. If you want to see the new JPEG version, you have to open that file.

   You can actually adjust the pixel count in the Save for Web dialog box as well, so you can resize and save your original image in the JPEG format all in one step if you choose. Make the pixel count change using the Image Size area of the dialog box. First, select the Constrain Proportions box and enter either the new pixel width or height. Then click the Apply button to dump those unneeded pixels. From that point, just follow the preceding steps to set the JPEG file-saving options.

Sharing Photos on Removable Media

A computer with an Internet connection replaces the photo albums and slide shows of yesteryear. All you need to enjoy your pictures these days is the Web address of your photo host.

Still, other ways are available to share photos with family and friends. You can copy your pictures to a CD, DVD, or flash drive that you can carry with you or mail to someone else. *Flash drives* are thumb-sized or smaller devices that plug into a computer's USB port. Copying files to and deleting files from a flash drive is often easier than doing those same tasks on a CD or DVD.

You can arrange the photos you copy (or *burn*) to these types of removable media in several different ways:

- ✔ As data files
- ✔ In a slide show
- ✔ As a video

Which method is better for you depends in part on the effort you want to make in the creation of the disk. Another factor is whether you want the disk to be played on a computer or a DVD player connected to a television.

 When you travel with a laptop, take extra cables (USB and RCA) along so that you can hook the laptop to a TV or DVD player for a great way to show your photos. Some DVD players even connect to USB flash drives.

Copying photos to a disk or drive as data

Digital photos are files just like any other electronic data. Consequently, you can copy those files to any disk through the common process of copy and paste or drag and drop.

Most computers can read a CD, DVD, or flash drive created this way. How the photos are displayed by the recipient of this disk or flash drive is really up to him or her. When you drop separate image files to a disk or flash drive, they show up as just a bunch of files — not as a slide show. The viewer decides which pictures to view or skip, and in any order.

 You might consider renaming the image files on the disk or flash drive so that when they are viewed as a list, they are also organized in the order you want them viewed (usually chronological). Because filenames are generally listed in alphabetical order, the three files morning.jpg, afternoon.jpg, and evening.jpg are likely to be listed as afternoon, evening, and morning on-screen. But if you rename these files to picture01.jpg (originally, morning.jpg), picture02.jpg (originally, afternoon.jpg), and picture03.jpg (originally, evening.jpg), they should appear in the order you want them viewed — unless the viewer sorts them differently. Another sorting option is to sort by the time taken. But if you sorted the three pictures in this example in descending order by date and time taken, they would appear in reverse of the order you intended.

 Keep in mind that older television DVD players may not be able to read computer data disks. Newer television DVD players are likely to be compatible with newer computer DVD drives. You have the convergence between entertainment and computing industries to thank for that.

Burning photos as a slide show

Rather than simply copy separate image files to a CD, DVD, or flash drive, you can organize your photos into a slide show presentation. Such a slide show can include transitions between photos, including text on or between photos, and you can even play music during the show. But don't panic: These slide shows can actually be easy and fun to create.

The main advantage of a slide show over treating the photos as data files (as discussed in the preceding section) is that you control the order in which the slides are viewed. And you can repeatedly revise this order as you go.

Your computer may have come with software that lets you create slide shows, or the software may be freely available from the provider of your Internet service. If not, your photo organizer or editor may have a slide show feature. (For free slide show software, see the shareware editor at www.irfanview.com.)

Figure 1-20 shows Windows DVD Maker (included with the Home Premium and Ultimate editions of Windows Vista) with Add Items and Duration (how long to keep the image on-screen) circled in red. After you select all the photos you want to include in your slide show, you select a theme for the slide show control menus and for the slide show background. When you are ready, you click the Burn button.

The person viewing the slide show can start, pause, and stop the slide show at will. A separate menu enables the viewer to see individual slides separately from the show.

Not all television DVD players can execute a computer slide show, which is a computer program, although they may still allow the viewer to pick through the photos.

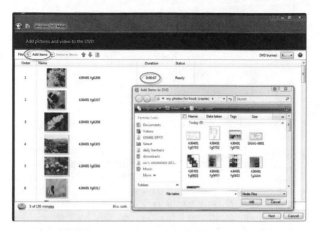

Figure 1-20: Add items and arrange them in a slide show, as shown here with Windows DVD Maker.

Creating a photo video

You can also create one single, large video file out of the many individual photos (and video and audio files) you want to share. This video can provide more transitions and special effects than a standard slide show. All the control over what is seen when and for how long rests with the creator of the video. The viewer simply watches.

Slide shows and videos of photos look similar as they play, although one key difference is that a video is a single, large file, whereas a slide show consists of separate files for each photo. Also, video-editing software provides many more effects and transitions than most slide show software.

Your computer may have come with software to create videos out of photos. If not, your photo organizer or editor may provide this feature. (For free video-creation or editing software, see the shareware editor at www.irfanview.com.)

Figure 1-21 shows a video being created using Windows Movie Maker (included with the Home Premium and Ultimate editions of Windows Vista). You can import photos, other images, videos, and music to your video project. You can add transitions between media and effects to each item on the Storyboard, which you can see at the bottom of Figure 1-21.

When you're ready, you can publish the video to the computer or to a CD or DVD (see the options circled in red in Figure 1-21). To create a video you intend to copy to a flash drive, use the This Computer option. The software you use may also offer options to specify the quality of the video, which directly affects its file size — better quality means a bigger file. The E-mail option shown in the left pane creates a smaller video file for attaching to e-mail. If you're uploading to a video service, however, you may want to go for better quality and not worry so much about the file size.

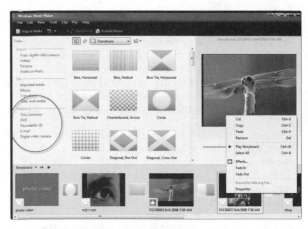

Figure 1-21: Video-creation tools include more transitions and effects than simpler slide shows.

Chapter 2

Printing and Scanning Your Photos

● ●

In This Chapter

▶ Reviewing your printing options

▶ Choosing a photo printer

▶ Printing your own photos

▶ Getting better monitor-to-printer color matching

▶ Making black-and-white prints

▶ Printing photo albums

● ●

*G*etting a grip on all there is to know about digital photography can be a little overwhelming — we know, we've been there. So if you're feeling like your head is already about to pop from all the new terms and techniques you've stuffed into it, we have great news for you: You need to read only the first section of this chapter to find out how to get terrific prints of your digital photos.

Those first paragraphs introduce you to retail photo-printing services that make getting digital prints easy, fast, and amazingly inexpensive. If you like, you can handle the whole thing via the Internet, without ever leaving home.

When you're ready for do-it-yourself printing — and that process, too, has been greatly simplified since the first days of digital photography — the rest of the chapter offers tips on buying a photo printer and getting the best results from it. And whether you're printing your own photos or letting someone else do the honor, this chapter also discusses ways to get your printed colors to match what you see on your monitor (or closer to that goal, anyway).

Printing from a Lab

 In the first years of digital photography, the only option for people who didn't want to print their own photos was to find a professional photo lab that could handle digital files. Unless you lived in a major city, you probably didn't have access to such a lab, and if you did, you paid big bucks to get your prints.

Now, any outlet that offers film developing, from your local drugstore to big-box retailers such as Costco or Wal-Mart, also offers quick and easy digital photo processing. You just take your camera memory card to the store and specify what pictures you want to print. Depending on the service and the specific store, you can have the staff handle everything for you or upload your photos at a special kiosk and input your desired sizes, paper selections, and quantities. You can also do this online from the comfort of your own home, if you like; you simply upload the photos onto the store's photo Web site.

The cost of retail printing continues to get less expensive, too. Depending on the number of prints you make, you can get 4 x 6-inch prints for as little as

17 cents apiece, and spend as little as $1.49 for an 8 x 10-inch print. And remember, the only prints you pay for are those you choose to upload, as opposed to how things worked in film days, when you paid to print the entire roll, including the pictures that didn't turn out so great.

You have a variety of options for getting your digital prints:

- ✔ **One-hour printing:** Take in your memory card, leave instructions about your print job, and go run other errands or do your shopping. Come back in an hour and pick up your prints.

  If you're worried about a lab losing your memory card, by the way, you usually have the option of copying your pictures to a CD or some other removable media, such as one of those tiny flash memory keys, and taking that to the photo lab. Just make sure that the lab can accept the type of media you want to use.

- ✔ **Instant-print kiosks:** In a hurry? You may not even need to wait an hour for those prints. Many stores have kiosks that can print your pictures immediately. Again, you just put in your memory card, push a few buttons, and out come your prints. You can even do some retouching, such as cropping and eliminating red-eye, right at the kiosk.

- ✔ **Order online, print locally:** You can send your image files via the Internet to most retail photo printers and then specify the store where you want your prints made. Then pick up the prints at your convenience.

This option also makes it easy to get prints to faraway friends and relatives. Instead of having the prints made at your local lab and then mailing them off, you can simply upload your files to a lab near the people who want the prints. They can then pick up the prints at that lab. You can either prepay with a credit card or have the person getting the prints pay upon picking them up.

For help finding a lab that's conveniently located, check out www.takegreatpictures.com, which is provided by the Photo Marketing Association and lists lots of locations by Zip code. (Look for the Find a Photo Lab link.) Or, you can go directly to the Web sites of major retailers, such as Wal-mart or Costco, and find a list of printing services offered at each one. (Note that to use the Costco service, you have to be a Costco member.)

✔ **Order online, get prints by mail:** Some major retailers also offer this option. In addition, you can order prints by mail from online photo-sharing sites such as Kodak Gallery (www.kodakgallery.com), Snapfish (www.snapfish.com), and Shutterfly (www.shutterfly.com).

Buying a Photo Printer

Even if you have most of your prints made at a retail lab, adding a photo printer to your digital-photography system is still a good investment, for several reasons:

✔ When you need only a print or two, it's more convenient to do the job yourself than to send the pictures to a lab.

- ✔ For times when you're feeling artistic, you can print on special media, such as canvas-textured paper. With a model such as the $150 HP Photosmart D7460, shown in Figure 2-1, you can even output borderless prints in sizes up to 8.5 x 24 inches.

- ✔ Doing your own printing gives you complete control over the output, which is important to many photo enthusiasts, especially those who exhibit or sell their work.

- ✔ Today's photo printers can produce excellent results. In fact, most people can't tell the difference between prints made at home and those made at a lab.

Hewlett-Packard

Figure 2-1: With this HP D7460 printer, you can output borderless inkjet prints up to 8.5 x 24 inches.

When you go printer shopping, you'll encounter several types of printers. Each offers advantages and disadvantages, and the technology you choose depends on your budget, your printing needs, and your print-quality expectations. To help you make sense of things, the following sections discuss the three main types of consumer and small-office printers.

Inkjet printers

Inkjet printers work by forcing little drops of ink through nozzles onto the paper. Inkjet printers designed for the home office or small business cost anywhere from $50 to $1,300.

Inkjets fall into three basic categories:

- **General-purpose models:** These printers are engineered to do a decent job on both text and pictures, but are sometimes geared more to text and document printing than photos.

- **Photo printers:** Sometimes referred to as *photo-centric* printers, these models are designed with the digital photographer in mind and usually produce better-quality photographic output than all-purpose printers. But they're sometimes not well suited to everyday text printing because the print speed can be slower than on a general-purpose machine. They also require more individual ink cartridges and may only output small, snapshot-size images. However, many printers do have a foot in both the general-purpose and photo printer camps, offering good results for all printing uses.

- **Multi-purpose printers:** These models combine a printer with a flatbed scanner (which can also be used as a document copier) and sometimes also a fax machine. So you can print an image file or scan a printed photo and turn it into a digital file — and then print it again! Figure 2-2 shows one all-in-one model, the Epson Stylus Photo RX680. This particular machine can even print directly onto printable CDs and DVDs, so you can label your own disks. Today, many multi-purpose printers offer great photo-printing abilities, but some are more business oriented and are engineered more to document printing.

Seiko Epson

Figure 2-2: The Epson Stylus Photo RX680 is a scanner, copier, and photo printer that also prints onto CDs and DVDs.

Typically, photo-printing quality peaks as you reach the $150 price range, though. Higher-priced inkjets offer speedier printing and extra features, such as the following:

- ✔ Ability to print on wide-format paper (larger than the usual 8½ x 11-inch letter size)
- ✔ More than four ink cartridges, for better color rendering
- ✔ Borderless printing
- ✔ Computer-network connections
- ✔ Wireless Bluetooth connections

✔ Printing directly from a camera or memory card

✔ Built-in monitors that you can use to preview your pictures

✔ Integrated fax, copier, and scanner

Most inkjet printers enable you to print on plain paper or thicker (and more expensive) photographic stock, either with a glossy or matte finish. That flexibility is great because you can print rough drafts and everyday work on plain paper and save the more costly photographic stock for final prints and important projects.

The downside? Well, you've no doubt discovered this for yourself: Although most inkjet printers themselves are inexpensive, *printing* is not necessarily cheap because the inks they use can be pretty pricey. And inkjet printer manufacturers will almost always tell you that you need to use their own brand of ink instead of less-costly third-party inks.

Another option is to have your inkjet cartridges professionally refilled at a local store; this service is becoming common, especially in large metropolitan areas. The vendors guarantee the quality of the ink, and if you don't like the results, you have a place you can go to with your prints to get help.

Either way, using a third-party, aftermarket brand of ink, while less expensive and sometimes perfectly adequate, can *potentially* produce unsatisfactory results and, worse yet, can invalidate your warranty. So beware before buying a bunch of cheap inkjet cartridges, do your homework by researching the topic to see what other users of your printer have experienced. And do stop to consider that printer manufacturers spend lots of research time and money developing ink formulas that best mesh with their printers' ink delivery systems and with various papers, including those they manufacture and sell themselves. So it does make sense that the media offered by the manufacturer — both inks and papers — would stand the best chance of producing optimum results.

All that said, inkjets are the best option for most digital photographers. The exception is if you have high-volume printing needs or care as much about regular document printing as photo printing. If that describes you, check out laser printers, too, described next. And if you're interested only in printing snapshot photos — perhaps you already have a printer for outputting letters and other documents — the upcoming section about dye-sub printers may also be of interest.

Laser printers

Laser printers use a technology similar to that used in photocopiers. You probably don't care to know the details, so here's the general idea: The process involves a laser beam, which produces electric charges on a drum, which rolls toner — the ink, if you will — onto the paper. Heat is applied to the page to permanently affix the toner to the page.

The upsides to laser printers include:

✔ Color lasers can produce near-photographic quality images as well as excellent text.

✔ They're faster than inkjets.

- ✔ You can use plain paper or special photo paper, just as with an inkjet (although you get better results if you use a high-grade laser paper as opposed to cheap copier paper).

- ✔ Although you may pay more up front for a laser printer than for an inkjet, you should save money over time because the price of toner is usually lower than for inkjet ink.

- ✔ Many color lasers are designed for high-volume, networked printing, making them attractive to offices where several people share the same printer.

The downsides?

- ✔ Although they've become much more affordable over the past two years, color lasers still run $150 and up, with a much higher average price than inkjet printers (although prices are still going down).

- ✔ These printers tend to be big in stature as well as price — this typically isn't a machine that you want to use in a small home office that's tucked into a corner of your kitchen.

- ✔ Most laser printers don't have the digital-photography niceties found in many inkjets: memory-card slots, monitors for viewing photos on your cards, and the like. However, this situation is starting to change, with a few lasers now offering these and other photo-printing features.

As for photo quality, it varies from machine to machine, so be sure to read reviews carefully. Some laser-printed photos aren't quite as impressive as those from the best inkjets, but some new models come very close. Many people can't tell the difference between an inkjet and laser print. Figure 2-3 offers an example of a color laser printer from Konica Minolta.

Konica Minolta Photo Imaging

Figure 2-3: Color lasers are now very affordable and can produce good photo prints.

Dye-sub (thermal dye) printers

A third type of printer you may encounter, although it's not nearly as common as inkjets and laser printers, is called a *dye-sub* printer.

Dye-sub is short for *dye-sublimation,* which is worth remembering only for the purpose of one-upping the science-fair winner who lives down the street. Dye-sub printers transfer images to paper using a plastic film or ribbon that's coated with colored dyes. During the printing process, heating elements move across the film, causing the dye to fuse to the paper.

Dye-sub printers are also called *thermal-dye* printers — heated (thermal) dye . . . get it?

Some popular snapshot printers, including certain models from Kodak, use this technology. Dye-sub printers fall within the same price range as quality inkjets, and most produce good-looking prints.

Protecting your prints

No matter what the type of print, you can help keep its colors bright and true by adhering to the following storage and display guidelines:

✔ If you're framing the photo, mount it behind a matte to prevent the print from touching the glass. Be sure to use acid-free, archival matte board and UV-protective glass.

✔ Display the picture in a location where it isn't exposed to strong sunlight or fluorescent light for long periods of time.

✔ In photo albums, slip pictures inside acid-free, archival sleeves.

✔ Don't adhere prints to a matte board or other surface using masking tape, scotch tape, or other household products. Instead, use acid-free mounting materials, sold in art-supply stores and some craft stores. And don't write on the back of the print with anything but a pen made for printing on photographs.

✔ Limit exposure to humidity, wide temperature swings, cigarette smoke, and other airborne pollutants, as these can also contribute to image degradation. You can do this by having a framer "seal" the photo into a frame.

✔ Although the refrigerator door is a popular spot to hang favorite photos, it's probably the worst location in terms of print longevity. Unless protected by a frame, the photo paper soaks up all the grease and dirt from your kitchen, not to mention jelly-smudged fingerprints and other tell-tale signs left when people open and close the door.

✔ For the ultimate protection, always keep a copy of the image file on a CD-R, DVD-R, or other storage medium so that you can output a new print if the original one deteriorates.

However, dye-sub machines present a few disadvantages that may make them less appropriate as your primary home or office printer:

- ✔ Most dye-sub printers can output only snapshot size prints.

- ✔ You have to use special stock designed to work expressly with dye-sub printers. (Typically, you buy a printing pack that includes both the requisite paper and the dye film or ribbon.) That means that dye-sub printers aren't appropriate for general-purpose documents; these machines are purely photographic tools.

- ✔ Printing can be slower than with an inkjet or laser because the paper has to pass through the printer's innards several times, once for each color of dye and, usually, a final pass for the application of a clear overcoat.

More printer-shopping tips

After narrowing down what type and size of printer you need, a few additional shopping tips can help you pick the right product off the store shelves:

- ✔ **Don't spend on extras you won't use.** Decide whether you really need all the bells and whistles found on some new printers. For example, some will print directly onto a CD or DVD (although you need special but commonly available CDs or DVDs that accept inkjet ink printing), print from a wireless Bluetooth connection, or let you print directly from a memory card. These features may be handy for you, but if you don't need them, they will also make a printer more expensive than a similar-quality model without the extra whiz-bang features.

✔ **Don't worry too much about the specification known as *dpi*.** This abbreviation stands for *dots per inch* and refers to the number of dots of color the printer can create per linear inch. A higher dpi means a smaller printer dot, and the smaller the dot, the harder it is for the human eye to notice that the image is made up of dots. So in theory, a higher dpi should mean better-looking images. But because different types of printers create images differently, an image output at 300 dpi on one printer may look considerably better than an image output at the same or even higher dpi on another printer. And frankly, any new printer you buy today is probably going to offer enough resolution to produce print quality that's plenty good. So although printer manufacturers make a big deal about their printers' resolutions, dpi isn't always a reliable measure of print quality.

✔ **For inkjets, look for a model that uses four or more colors.** Most inkjets print using four colors: cyan, magenta, yellow, and black. This ink combination is known as CMYK (see the sidebar "The separate world of CMYK," later in this chapter). But some lower-end inkjets eliminate the black ink and just combine cyan, magenta, and yellow to approximate black. "Approximate" is the key word — you don't get good, solid blacks without that black ink, so for best color quality, avoid three-color printers.

Some high-end photo inkjets feature six or more ink colors, adding lighter shades of the primary colors or several shades of gray to the standard CMYK mix. The extra inks expand the range of colors that the printer can manufacture, resulting in more accurate color rendition, but add to the print cost.

If you enjoy making black-and-white prints —
grayscale prints, in official digital-imaging lingo —
look for a printer that adds the extra gray
cartridges. Some printers that use only one black
cartridge have a difficult time outputting truly
neutral grays — prints often have a slight color
tint. Browse magazines that cover black-and-
white photography for leads on the best
machines for this type of printing.

✔ **Inkjets that use separate cartridges for each
color save you money.** On models that have
just one cartridge for all inks, you usually end
up throwing away some ink because one color
often becomes depleted before the others. With
multiple ink cartridges, you just replace the
ones that are running out.

A few printers require special cartridges for
printing in photographic-quality mode. These
cartridges are normally more expensive than
standard inks. So when you compare output
from different printers, find out whether the
images were printed with the standard ink
setup or with more expensive photographic
inks.

In some cases, these cartridges lay down a
clear overcoat over the printed image. The
overcoat gives the image a glossy appearance
when printed on plain paper and also helps
protect the ink from smearing and fading. In
other cases, you put in a cartridge that enables
you to print with more colors than usual —
for example, if the printer usually prints
using four inks, you may insert a special
photo cartridge that enables you to print
using six inks.

✔ **Compare print speeds if you're a frequent printer.** If you use your printer for business purposes and you print a lot of images, be sure that the printer you pick can output images at a decent speed. And be sure to find out the per-page print speed for printing at the printer's *highest* quality setting. Most manufacturers list print speeds for the lowest-quality or draft-mode printing. When you see claims like "Prints at speeds *up to* . . . ," you know you're seeing the speed for the lowest-quality print setting.

✔ **"Computer-free printing" options give you extra flexibility.** Some printers can print directly from camera memory cards — no computer required. Several technologies enable this feature:

- *Built-in memory card slots*: You insert your memory card, use the printer's control panel to set up the print job, and press the Print button. Be sure that the printer offers card slots that are compatible with the type of memory card you use, though.

- *PictBridge:* This feature enables you to hook up your camera to your printer for direct printing. (Both the camera and the printer must offer PictBridge capabilities.)

- *DPOF (dee-poff)*: This acronym stands for *digital print order format* and enables you to select the images you want to print through your camera's user interface. The camera records your instructions on the memory card. Then, if you use a printer that has memory card slots, you put the card into a slot, and the printer reads and outputs your "print order." Again, both the camera and the printer must offer DPOF technology.

- *Wireless connections:* Manufacturers are offering a number of Bluetooth-enabled printers, too. If you use a Bluetooth cell phone that has a camera, you can send your pictures from the phone to the printer wirelessly.

Of course, direct printing takes away your chance to edit your pictures; you may be able to use camera or printer settings to make minor changes, such as rotating the image, making the picture brighter, or applying a prefab frame design, but that's all. Direct printing is great on occasions where print immediacy is more important than image perfection, however. For example, a real-estate agent taking a client for a site visit can shoot pictures of the house and output prints in a flash so that the client can take pictures home that day.

✔ **Research independent sources for cost-per-printer information.** Consumer magazines and computer publications often publish articles that compare current printer models based on cost per print. Some printers do use more expensive media than others, so if you're having trouble deciding between several similar models, this information could help you make the call. Note that some printer ads and brochures also state a cost per print, but the numbers you see are approximations at best and are calculated in a fashion designed to make the use costs appear as low as possible. As they say in the car ads, your actual mileage may vary.

✔ **Read reviews and blog comments for other input, too.** Once again, it pays to check out reviews in magazines and online sites to find detailed reviews about print quality and other printer features. You also can get lots of good real-world information by searching out blogs and user forums where people discuss their experiences with models that you're considering.

The separate world of CMYK

On-screen images are *RGB* images. RGB images are created by combining red, green, and blue light. Your digital camera and scanner also produce RGB images. Professional printing presses and most, but not all, consumer printers, on the other hand, create images by mixing four colors of ink — cyan, magenta, yellow, and black. Pictures created using these four colors are called *CMYK* images. (The *K* is used instead of *B* because black is called the *key* color in CMYK printing.)

You may be wondering why four primary colors are needed to produce colors in a printed image, while only three are needed for RGB images. (Okay, you're probably not wondering that at all, but go with it, will you?) The answer is that unlike light, inks are impure. Black is needed to help ensure that black portions of an image are truly black, not some muddy gray, as well as to account for slight color variations between inks produced by different vendors.

What does all this CMYK stuff mean to you? First, if you're shopping for an inkjet printer, be aware that some models print using only three inks, leaving out the black. Color rendition is usually worse on models that omit the black ink.

Second, if you're sending your image to a service bureau for printing, you may need to convert your image to the CMYK color mode and create *color separations*. CMYK images comprise four color channels — one each for the cyan, magenta, yellow, and black image information. Color separations are nothing more than grayscale printouts of each color channel. During the printing process, your printer combines the separations to create the full-color image. If you're not comfortable doing the CMYK conversion and color separations yourself or your image-editing software doesn't offer this capability, your service bureau or printer can do the job for you. (Be sure to ask the service rep whether you should provide RGB or CMYK images, because some printers require RGB.)

Don't convert your images to CMYK for printing on your own printer, however, because consumer printers are engineered to work with RGB image data. And no matter whether you're printing your own images or having them commercially reproduced, remember that CMYK has a smaller *gamut* than RGB, which is a fancy way of saying that you can't reproduce with inks all the colors you can create with RGB. CMYK can't handle the really vibrant, neon colors you see on your computer monitor, for example, which is why images tend to look a little duller after conversion to CMYK and why your printed images don't always match your on-screen images.

One more note about CMYK: If you're shopping for a new inkjet printer, you may see a few models described as CcMmYK or CcMmYKk printers. Those lowercase letters indicate that the printer offers a light cyan, magenta, or black ink, respectively, in addition to the traditional cyan, magenta, and black cartridges. As mentioned earlier, the added inksets are provided to expand the range of colors that the printer can produce.

Choosing Photo Paper

With photo paper, as with most things in life, you get what you pay for. The better the paper, the more your images will look like traditional print photographs. In fact, if you want to upgrade the quality of your images, simply changing the paper stock can do wonders.

If your printer can accept different stocks, print drafts of your images on the cheaper stocks, and reserve the good stuff for final output. "Good stuff," by the way, means photographic paper from a well-known manufacturer, not the cheap store brands. Start with paper from the manufacturer of your printer because that paper is specifically engineered to work with your printer's inks. The prints you make with that paper can give you a baseline from which you can compare results on other brands.

 Don't limit yourself to printing images on standard photo paper, though. You can buy special paper kits that enable you to put images on calendars, stickers, greeting cards, window decals, transparencies (for use in overhead projectors), and all sorts of other stuff. Some printers even offer accessory kits for printing your photos on coffee mugs and t-shirts. And if you use an inkjet printer, try out some of the new textured papers, which have surfaces that mimic traditional watercolor paper, canvas, and the like.

Setting Print Size and Resolution

As mentioned several times earlier in this chapter, many printers enable you to output prints right from a memory card or from the camera. If you're going that route, just follow the instructions in your printer manual. There's really not much to do in advance of printing except specify the size of the print and the number of copies, which you do either via your camera menus or buttons on the printer.

Many photo-editing programs also offer simplified printing, providing wizards that ask you to set only print size and other basics. If you like the results you get from these automated printing utilities, great. But keep in mind that when you set the print size this way, you let the printer software or your imaging software make the all-important resolution decision for you.

Here's a couple things to keep in mind:

- ✔ Resolution — pixels per inch — has a major impact on print quality. To do their best work, most printers need 200 to 300 pixels per inch. If you're having your picture output at a professional lab, you may be required to submit the file at a specific resolution.

- ✔ When you enlarge an image, one of two things happens: The resolution goes down and the pixel size increases, or the software adds new pixels to fill the enlarged image area (a process called *resampling*). Both options can result in a loss of image quality.

- ✔ To figure out the maximum size at which you can print your image at a desired resolution, divide the horizontal pixel count (the number of pixels across) by the desired resolution. The result gives you the maximum print width (in inches). To determine the maximum print height, divide the vertical pixel count by the desired resolution.

- ✔ What if you don't have enough pixels to get both the print size and resolution you want? Well, you have to choose which is more important. If you absolutely need a certain print size, you just have to sacrifice some image quality and accept a lower resolution. And if you absolutely need a certain resolution, you have to live with a smaller image. Hey, life's full of compromises, right?

Again, if you're happy with the prints you get when you go the automatic route, that's terrific. Some print utilities offer guidance as to how large you can print your picture without losing quality; pay attention to those on-screen messages, and you'll be fine.

But if you *do* want to take control over output resolution, you must set the print size and resolution *before* you send the image to the printer. Here's how to do the job in Elements:

1. **Choose Image⇨Resize⇨Image Size.**

   The Image Size dialog box shown in Figure 2-4 appears.

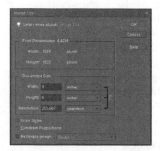

Figure 2-4: Set print size and output resolution (ppi) in the Image Size dialog box.

2. **Turn off the Resample Image check box.**

   This option controls whether the program can add or delete pixels as you change the print dimensions. When the option is turned off, the number of pixels can't be altered.

Click the box to toggle the option on and off. An empty box means that the option is turned off, which is what you want in this case.

3. Enter the print dimensions or resolution.

Enter the print dimensions in the Width or Height boxes; as you change one value, the other changes automatically to retain the original proportions of the picture. Likewise, as you change the dimensions, the Resolution value changes automatically. If you prefer, you can change the Resolution value, in which case the program alters the Width and Height values accordingly.

If you want your picture to print at a traditional photo size — say, 4 x 6 inches or 5 x 7 inches — you need to crop it to those proportions before you set the image size, depending on the proportions of your original digital image. Many cameras produce images that have a 4:3 aspect ratio, for example, which means that the entire image can't fit a 4 x 6 print size, which has an aspect ratio of 3:2.

Also note that for good print quality, you should strive for a resolution between 200 and 300. But you usually don't have to be dead-on with any particular resolution unless you're sending your photo to a lab that requires a specific value. (See the notes following these steps for details on how to handle that situation.)

4. Click OK or press Enter.

If you did things correctly — that is, deselected the Resample Image check box in Step 2 — you shouldn't see any change in your image on-screen, because you still have the same number of pixels to display. However, if you choose

View➪Rulers, which displays rulers along the top and left side of your image, you can see that the image will, in fact, print at the dimensions you specified.

5. If you want to retain the current settings after you close the image, save the file.

Now about that situation mentioned in Step 3: If you are sending your photo to a lab or for some other reason need to resample the image in order to achieve a certain print resolution, select the Resample Image check box. (Click the box so that a check mark appears inside.) Turn on the Constrain Proportions box and the Scale Styles box, if it's available. Then set your desired Width, Height, and Resolution values.

When the Resample Image option is enabled, a second set of Width and Height boxes becomes available at the top of the dialog box. Use these options if you want to set your photo dimensions using pixels or percent (of the original dimensions) as the unit of measure.

After resampling, be sure to *save your image with a new name.* You may want the image at the original pixel count some day.

If you're using another photo editor, be sure to consult the program's Help system or manual for information on resizing options available to you. Advanced photo-editing programs such as Elements offer you the option of controlling resolution as you resize, but some entry-level programs don't. Instead, these programs automatically resample the image any time you resize it, so be careful.

How can you tell if a program is resampling images upon resizing? Check the "before" and "after" size of the image file. If the file size changes when you resize the image, the program is resampling the photo. (Adding or deleting pixels increases or reduces the file size.)

Sending Your Image to the Printer

Printing from your photo-editing or cataloging software is similar to printing a file in any computer program. Here's the general overview:

1. **Open the photo file.**

2. **Set the image size and resolution as discussed in the preceding section.**

   If your photo software doesn't offer this capability, you can probably set the print size through the Printer dialog box, later in the steps. Setting the image size and resolution in the way discussed in the preceding section is a "best practices" type of thing, however.

3. **Choose the Print command.**

   In almost every program on the planet, the Print command resides on the File menu. Choosing the command results in a dialog box through which you can change the print settings, including the printer resolution or print quality and the number of copies you want to print. You can also specify whether you want to print in *portrait mode,* which prints your image in an upright position, or *landscape mode,* which prints your image sideways on the page. Figure 2-5 shows the dialog box that appears when you choose the Print command in Elements.

Figure 2-5: The Elements Print dialog box offers a variety of print settings.

4. **Specify the print options you want to use.**

   The available options — and the manner in which you access those options — vary widely depending on the type of printer you're using and whether you're working on a PC or a Mac.

   Please read your printer's manual for information on what settings to use in what scenarios, and, for heaven's sake, follow the instructions. Otherwise, you aren't going to get the best possible images your printer can deliver.

If you did establish print size and resolution before starting the print process, stay away from any options inside the Print dialog box that adjust the picture size or resolution, or you undo that work. In Elements, leave the Print Size option set to Actual Size, and keep your paws off the Scaled Print Size options.

5. **Send that puppy to the printer.**

   Look in the dialog box for an OK or Print button and click the button to send your image scurrying for the printer.

Getting better results from your printer

With the general printing info under your belt — and with your own printer manual close at hand — you're ready for some more specific tips about making hard copies of your images. So here are a few tips that can help you get the best output from any printer:

- ✔ **Better paper equals better prints.** For those special pictures, invest in glossy or "luster" photographic stock or some other high-grade option.

- ✔ **When setting up the print job, be sure to choose the right paper settings.** If the printer is set to print on matte paper, for example, and you instead feed it glossy stock, you might have a smeary mess on your hands.

- ✔ **Do a test print using different printer-resolution or print-quality settings.** This process enables you to determine which settings work best for which types of images and which types of paper.

The default settings selected by the printer's software may not be the best choices for the types of images you print. Be sure to note the appropriate settings so that you can refer to them later. Also, some printer software enables you to save custom settings so that you don't have to reset all the controls each time you print. Check your printer manual to find out whether your printer offers this option.

✔ **Don't forget to install the printer *driver* (software) on your computer.** Follow the installation instructions closely so that the driver is installed in the right folder in your system. Otherwise, your computer can't communicate with your printer. This is usually a matter of following the "quick setup" instructions that came with your printer. If you don't have them, you can usually find drive and setup files on the manufacturer's Web site (look for "downloads" and/or "support").

✔ **Use the right printer cable.** Most printers connect using a USB cable; if your printer didn't come with one, you can easily get one at a local office supply store. There are variations in quality, so don't just opt for the cheapest one. Also, remember that usually a longer cable means lessened performance, so try to work with a shorter printer cable, if possible.

✔ **Don't ignore your printer manual's instructions regarding routine printer maintenance.** Print heads can become dirty, inkjet nozzles can become clogged, and all sorts of other gremlins can gunk up the works. But don't get obsessive about it because the cleaning process consumes ink, costing you money as well as time.

As for the number-one printing complaint — printed colors that look different from on-screen colors — move to the next section.

Comparing your monitor to your prints

You may notice a significant color shift between your on-screen and printed images. This color shift is due in part to the fact that you simply can't reproduce all RGB colors using printer inks, a problem explained in the sidebar "The separate world of CMYK," earlier in this chapter. In addition, the following variables are at work:

- ✔ Brightness of the paper
- ✔ Purity of the ink
- ✔ Lighting conditions in which you view the image

Although perfect color matching is impossible, you can take a few steps to bring your printer and monitor colors closer together, as follows:

- ✔ On an inkjet printer, check your ink status. An empty or clogged ink cartridge is very often the culprit when colors are seriously off.

- ✔ Changing your paper stock sometimes affects color rendition. Typically, the better the paper, the truer the color matching.

- ✔ The software provided with most color printers includes color-matching controls designed to get your screen and image colors to jibe. Check your printer manual for information on how to access these controls.

✔ If playing with the color-matching options doesn't work, the printer software may offer controls that enable you to adjust the image's color balance. When you adjust the color balance using the printer software, you don't make any permanent changes to your image. Again, you need to consult your printer manual for information on specific controls and how to access and use them.

✔ Don't convert your images to the CMYK color model for printing on a consumer printer. These printers are designed to work with RGB images, so you get better color matching if you work in the RGB mode.

✔ Many image-editing programs also include utilities that are designed to assist in the color-matching process. Some of these are very user-friendly; after printing a sample image, you let the program know which sample most closely matches what you see on-screen. The program then calibrates itself automatically using this information.

✔ Photoshop Elements, Photoshop, ACDSee, and other advanced image-editing programs offer more sophisticated color-management options. If you're new to the game, leave these settings in their default positions, as the whole topic is a little mind-boggling, and you can just as easily make things worse as improve them. Many of the color settings aren't designed to improve matching between your printer and monitor, anyway, but to ensure color consistency through a production workflow — that is, between different technicians passing an image file along from creation to printing.

✔ If your photography work demands more accurate color-matching controls than your printer or photo-editing software delivers, you can invest in a *color management system,* or CMS, for short. Incorporating special software and hardware tools, a CMS enables you to calibrate all the different components of your image-processing system — scanner, monitor, and printer — so that colors stay true from machine to machine. Among companies offering color-management products for consumers are Colorvision (www.colorvision.com) and X-Rite (www.xrite.com).

Even if you don't fully get into color management, you might consider picking up a *monitor calibration tool.* This little bit of hardware, which you can buy for about $100, measures the colors and brightness emitted by your monitor and then builds a profile that gets passed onto your computer, printer, and other imaging devices. In addition to adjusting the display to compensate for any inherent color cast it may have, the profile helps the other devices more accurately translate the colors in your image as they move from camera to monitor to printer.

✔ Finally, remember that the colors you see both on-screen and on paper vary depending on the light in which you view them. It is best to do this in a room with a limited amount of light shining on your screen. Additionally, the color of your clothing and even the surrounding walls can reflect off the monitor, causing more color confusion. So you may even want to don gray or black clothing when you're doing color-critical work.

Seeing Things in Black and White

While most of the pictures people take today are in color, you can easily change them to black and white using an image-editing program. Photoshop Elements, for example, has an easy-to-use tool for just this task, shown in Figure 2-6. And with many images, such as the photo in Figure 2-6, you may discover that you like the black-and-white version of some pictures better than the color original.

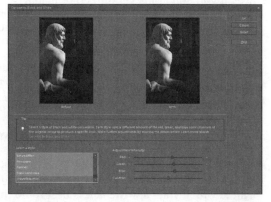

Serge Timacheff

Figure 2-6: Photoshop Elements makes converting color images to black-and-white easy.

After you do your conversion, save your image with a different filename using the Save As option (usually found under the File menu on your editing program). This ensures that you will have your original image *and* your new black-and-white version.

Printing your black-and-white images can be a challenge, though, because most photo printers are designed more for color printing. So follow these tips to get the best reproduction:

- ✔ A printer that uses two or more shades of black ink as well as the usual color inks produces the best results. Epson, Canon, and HP all offer a number of dedicated photo printers that use either two or three shades of black ink and are capable of printing great looking black and white prints. These printers are more expensive, however, and can sell for $800 and up.

- ✔ Paper matters, too. There are a number of inkjet papers with a variety of coatings and textures made specifically for monochrome (black-and-white) images, and using these products can make a big difference.

- ✔ If you can't get good results from your own printer, the easiest solution is to look for a lab that offers black-and-white printing. Labs that work with professional photographers, especially, offer various options, so check around — especially if you're printing an important photo that you are going to frame or have around for a long time.

Publishing Your Own Coffee Table Book

Ever seen a coffee-table-style book of photographs from a wedding? It used to be that you had to print copies of the best photos from a wedding or other event and then insert them into a leather- or linen-bound fancy book to keep as a high-quality showpiece.

Today, you can do the same thing online by uploading your favorite photos from virtually any event or collection and have them printed in a beautiful book like the one shown in Figure 2-7. You can have anywhere from a few photos to several hundred in a single book. And, as an added bonus, you can even create "virtual" copies of the book for sharing online, complete with music.

Many companies offer photo printing into books of all sizes and styles, including the following:

Amy A. Timacheff

Figure 2-7: Photobooks are easy to produce online and have printed for a high-quality keepsake from weddings, graduations, and other events.

- ✔ Picaboo (www.picaboo.com)
- ✔ Shutterfly (www.shutterfly.com)
- ✔ Lulu (www.lulu.com)

✔ Snapfish (www.snapfish.com)

✔ Kodak Gallery (www.kodakgallery.com)

You simply create an online account, decide on a design, upload your photos, and then use the various templates and layouts provided to create your book.

For something on a smaller scale, you can create a mini album like the one shown in Figure 2-8. This product, from ZoomAlbum (www.zoomalbum.net), is only 3 inches square — perfect for carrying in your pocket to your next supper club or family reunion. You typically can create an album on a single sheet of paper (provided with the kit) and your own printer. You then peel the photos from a special backing and stick them into the album cover. A kit that makes about three albums sells for around $30.

ZoomAlbum, Inc.

Figure 2-8: ZoomAlbums are 3-inch photo albums you can make at home and take anywhere.

Scanning Prints

The convenience of having photos in digital form to view and share suggests that older prints may find new life in digital form. You can digitize printed material using a *scanner*, a device that *scans* the original and turns it into an electronic file (and people say computer lingo is hard).

When scanners were invented in the previous century, the developers also (indirectly) created one of the funniest computer acronyms: TWAIN. New scanners were said to be TWAIN-compliant. TWAIN was interpreted to stand for Technology Without An Interesting Name. That's almost as good as PCMCIA: People Can't Memorize Computer Industry Acronyms. (On the contrary.)

We digress . . . to scan your prints to digital format, you need both hardware and software:

✔ **Hardware:** The scanner is the hardware you connect to your computer, usually by USB. Unless space or portability is an issue, get a *flatbed* scanner large enough to handle the prints you want to scan. A flatbed scanner lets you lay the full image flat on the machine. With a *handheld* scanner, on the other hand, you hold the device in your hand and run it over the piece you are scanning. It may work adequately, but it won't be as convenient or easy to use.

The scanner has a range of resolution. If you're expecting to view the scans only on-screen, the low end of the range is fine (100 to 300 dpi). High-resolution scans above 1200 dpi produce very large files. This resolution might be desirable if you plan to print a new large print. (In this case, consider carefully photographing the original print instead of scanning it.)

✔ **Software:** Scanning software comes with the scanner, although other software is available. The big issue in scanning printed matter is whether you want the resulting file to be an image or you want the text recognized as text. Clearly, you want image files from your photo prints.

If you want to have one machine that does it all, look into the so-called multifunction or all-in-one printers that include a scanner, color printer, copier, and fax.

Figure 2-9 shows a dialog box from scanning software. Current settings are circled, and the arrow points to the Resolution menu item. You can adjust many settings through menus; you can also adjust the resulting scan file through your photo editor.

Figure 2-9: Preview a scan and make any adjustments before completing the scan.

Rather than remove photos from album pages, try scanning the entire page, if it fits your scanner. Using your photo editor after the scan, you can crop the individual photos out of the single scan, rotate them as needed, and more.

For photos currently in stacks or envelopes, arrange as many as will fit on the scanner plate, scan them, and then crop the individual photos from the single scan. Scanning a bunch together and cropping each photo later is usually faster than scanning individual photos.

You can save your scans as JPEGs or TIFFs. JPEGs are smaller and easier to share. TIFFs are larger and may be better for editing or printing. Are you planning to make new prints from old ones? Or is the point of scanning your photos to enable you to switch to the convenience of digital photos? You'll likely find that JPEGs are more convenient than TIFFs.

Upload scans of old family photos to a photo-sharing service to share with the whole family in new digital albums.

Chapter 3

Enjoying Digital Picture Frames

* *

In This Chapter

▶ Selecting a digital picture frame

▶ Setting up your picture frame

▶ Displaying photos from your camera's memory card

▶ Changing frame settings

▶ Editing photos for frames

▶ Copying photos from your computer

* *

Digital picture frames give you another option for enjoying and sharing your photos. A digital picture frame presents a continuous slideshow. You can display your photos in your home or office without needing a computer.

Digital frames may soon replace the photo albums of yesteryear. One frame, using a memory card from your camera or computer, may hold hundreds of photos. With a push of a button, thumbnails display to allow you to pick a photo to fill the screen. Other buttons enable you to flip through your photos as easily as flipping the pages of an album.

The number of frame manufacturers and models has increased tremendously in just a few years. At the same time, good frames cost less than ever. Unfortunately, choosing a frame is complicated by a wide variation in features, as you see in this chapter.

You may find good deals on frames online, but it is very hard to judge a frame without seeing it in use. Visit an office supply or discount electronics store to compare frames. Figure 3-1 shows two frames.

Slight padding on edges for cropped photo

Clock

Figure 3-1: Digital frames come in many styles.

After you have your frame, you can insert a memory card directly from your camera. If you have a computer, you can copy photos from it to a flash drive or memory card to use in your frame.

Selecting a Digital Picture Frame

As with cameras, there are many features to consider when shopping for a digital picture frame. A few of these features are essential considerations, whereas other features may be less important to you.

 If you have access to a computer, search the Web for digital picture frame reviews. One good site is www.digitalpictureframereview.com. You'll also find many consumer comments at www.amazon.com.

Among the most important considerations are the following:

- ✔ **Screen dimensions:** The display area of a frame is usually smaller than the overall dimensions of the frame, which includes a border or mat that may be anywhere from less than an inch around up to a few inches. A large frame may have a small display area. The display area is measured diagonally in inches. A 7" display area is comparable to a standard 4 x 6 print. A display area 7" or smaller might be ideal on a desk or by the phone. For a frame that will sit on a table or shelf, 8" or greater may be better. Frames with a display area greater than 10" are more expensive and tend to have more features than many people need.

- ✔ **Screen resolution:** Resolution is measured in pixels (dots) for width and height. High resolution is indicated by bigger numbers. Good resolution ranges from 800 x 600 to 1024 x 768. Resolutions below that range may not be sharp enough.

As you compare two frames, consider both the diagonal measure and the resolution. If two frames have the same diagonal measurement, the one with the higher resolution should be sharper and clearer.

✔ **Aspect ratio:** Your eyes may glaze over at this term, but it is no less important than the preceding features. *Aspect ratio* refers to width versus height. Most digital cameras take photos with a 4:3 aspect ratio. (That's the same ratio as TV before digital.) Both 800 x 600 and 1024 x 768 are 4:3, which makes those resolutions ideal for most digital photos. Some frames display photos at a higher ratio of 16:9, which is wider than the other ratio. (That's the same ratio as high-definition digital TV.) When a photo with one ratio displays on a frame with another ratio, something's gotta give. Most frames put black borders around part of a photo to make the adjustment, padding the difference in width or height. Some frames may adjust the photo to fit the frame if the photo and frame have different aspect ratios. If the frame adjusts the photo, there is a chance for distortion or for the edges of the photo to be cut off. Look for frames with the 4:3 aspect ratio or, if your camera and frame both have 16:9, set your camera to that option in the setup menus.

Regardless of aspect ratio, portrait photos fit oddly in landscape frames, and vice versa, although most people don't set the frame up in portrait orientation. In most cases, black bars appear left and right of the portrait to fill the width. Live with this or avoid putting portraits on your frame.

✔ **Memory card slots:** Frames accept camera memory cards so that you can display photos from the same card you use to take photos. Make sure the frame you buy reads the same card you use in your camera. Most frames read more than one type of card. If your frame and camera use different cards, you can use a computer to prepare photos for the frame. For more on that, see the section "Copying Photos from Your Computer."

Along with the preceding features, consider a few more as you compare frames:

✔ **Brightness:** A bright screen shows off your photos in their best light. Although specifications may help in comparing frames, it is difficult to judge brightness without seeing a frame in use.

✔ **Contrast ratio:** Contrast is the difference between light and dark areas on the screen. The greater the ratio (for example, 300:1), the better.

✔ **Viewing angle:** This feature refers to how far off-center you can stand or sit and still clearly see the photo. An extremely narrow viewing angle requires you to be directly in front of the frame to see your photos. A wide horizontal viewing angle lets more people gather around a frame and see photos equally well. When you are beyond the viewing angle of any screen, the photo is unrecognizable. The vertical viewing angle becomes more significant if you intend to place the frame on a low table or a high shelf. Theoretically, a 180 degree vertical viewing angle and a 180 degree horizontal viewing angle would be perfect — you could see it standing off to the side. Many frames have a viewing angle of less than 90 degrees in either direction.

✔ **Internal memory:** Not all frames have internal or built-in memory for storing photos. Those that do have memory vary in how much they have. The more internal memory a frame has, the more pictures it can store without using a memory card. However, you may choose to store your photos on removable memory cards. In that case, you may not need much or any internal memory.

✔ **Controls:** All frames have buttons and switches for power, menus, and moving from one picture to the next. These controls are often on the back of the frame or the sides. Some frames have touch screens, either on the display area or in the frame outside the display area. The size and location of these controls, and the effort required to press them, affects ease of use. Some controls are very slow to respond and require a firm press and patience. This is another feature you can only judge by using it.

One downside of touch screens is that most show fingerprints and smudges. See Figure 3-2. A remote control frees you from touching the frame to change photos or settings. If a frame comes with a remote, make sure it's not too small to use easily.

Here are some other features you may consider important:

✔ **Audio speakers:** Do you want to play music on your frame? Will you play videos with sound? If not, speakers don't matter.

✔ **Battery power:** All frames plug in for power. If you want to use a frame as a portable photo album to pass around, look for one that uses rechargeable batteries, as well.

✔ **Clock or calendar:** Many frames have built-in clocks. Some let you set alarms. Some frames have calendars. You may be able to display the time or a calendar next to your photos.

Some frames let you schedule times to turn the frame on and off to save power.

✔ **Frame style:** Some frames are sleekly modern with glossy plastic or metal. Others imitate traditional photo frames with wood. Some come with extra faceplates or mats to change the color of the area outside the display area.

Smudges   Fingerprints

Figure 3-2: This frame's been handled by many people, and it shows.

✔ **In-frame editing:** Basic editing includes rotating a portrait into vertical position and cropping to emphasize the subject by removing the surrounding area in the photo. If you have a computer, you may find it more convenient to edit on the computer than by using the frame's functions for editing. Your camera may also have some basic editing features.

✔ **USB connections:** Some frames accept USB flash drives as an easy way to transfer photos from a computer. (Ads may refer to the frame as a *USB host*, in this case.) Separately, most frames accept a USB cable to connect directly to a computer to transfer photos. This requires taking the frame to the computer and also plugging in the frame's own power cord, unless the frame runs on batteries.

✔ **Video format:** Do you want to play movies on your frame? Compare the format your camera records with the formats the frame can play.

✔ **Wireless connectivity:** A wireless function allows a computer to send photos directly to a frame without wires. Photos can even come from friends and family over the Internet. Unfortunately, this can be tricky to configure, so don't get this feature unless you have experience with wirelessly networking computers or know someone who does.

Small laptop computers may be a suitable alternative to a digital picture frame. An 8" *netbook* may cost two or three times as much as a frame, but you'll get more, including photo organizing and editing functions, as well as Internet connectivity. When you want your laptop to act like a frame, start a slideshow.

Setting Up Your Picture Frame

Setting up your frame for the first time is pretty easy.
Just follow these steps:

1. **Unpack the parts from the box.**

   Keep all packing material until you are certain
   you won't need to return the frame. Identify the
   frame, stand, and the power supply.

2. **Attach the stand to the frame.**

   Some stands insert, clip, or screw onto an area
   on the back of the frame. Some frames have different connections depending on whether you
   want the frame horizontal (landscape) or vertical
   (portrait). Set the frame up for horizontal display,
   unless most of the photos you intend to display
   are portraits. See Figure 3-3.

Power switch

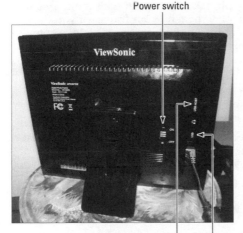

USB host for flash drive   USB for computer

Figure 3-3: The rear of the digital frame.

3. **Put the frame in a spot safe from pets and traffic, within a cord's length of a wall plug.**

4. **Connect the power supply to the frame on the back or side.**

5. **Plug the frame into the wall.**

6. **Turn the frame on.**

   The power switch is a button or slider on the side or back of the frame. The frame's logo and a screen with information on switches appear on some models. A demo slideshow starts automatically. See the section "Displaying Photos from Your Camera's Memory Card."

Displaying Photos from Your Camera's Memory Card

If you have photos on your camera's memory card, you can display them on your frame. (If you don't have any photos on the memory card, take some.) Follow these steps

1. **Turn the camera off and eject the memory card.**

   When you eject the card, note how the card was inserted originally. If you have a spare memory card, insert it into the camera.

   If you have two or more memory cards, one can be in the camera and another in the frame at all times.

2. **If the frame is on, turn it off.**

3. **Locate the appropriate slot for your memory card.**

   Most frames use combination slots that take more than one type of card. Wide slots make it trickier to insert the card correctly than in a camera. Metal contacts go in first. Insert the card gently.

Don't push the card in beyond the edge of the slot or you may have trouble removing the card. (Try using tweezers if your card gets stuck.) If the card does not slide easily into place, pull it out and turn it over and try again or look for another slot. Be gentle: Do not force the card or pull it out too strongly.

4. **Turn the frame on.**

   A menu may appear at first, but after a moment, most frames begin to show photos from the memory card.

Changing Frame Settings

To change your frame's settings, follow these steps

1. **If the frame is off, turn it on.**

   If you normally use a memory card, leave that card inserted in the frame.

2. **Locate the Menu or Setup button and press it.**

   This may be on the back, side, or front. You also need to identify the OK button (it may be the same as the Menu button) and other buttons that move the selection highlight up, down, left, and right.

3. **Use the appropriate button to move the selection highlight over Settings or Setup. Press the OK button to begin setup.**

   Look for a Settings or Setup option on the menu, which is sometimes represented by a gear or wrench. The menu may also include options to select a source for pictures. The picture source is usually selected automatically based on which card is inserted.

   Your frame may have some but not all of these options. Some options may appear only after you select another option:

   • **Frequency or interval:** How often do you want a new photo to appear? Choices may range from a few seconds to 24 hours. Choose 30 seconds or a minute to start. At an interval of 5 seconds or less, photos fly by. If you set the interval too long, you may feel impatient waiting for the photo to change. Some frames have Next and Previous buttons on the frame or remote to enable you to switch photos without waiting for the automatic interval to pass.

   • **Order:** Random order offers the most surprise. However, if your photos tell a story that progresses with each photo, choose something other than random. Other ordering options include by filename and by date taken.

   • **Effects or transitions:** Transition effects create a show as one photo replaces another. Without transitions, one photo disappears and the next replaces it instantly. With a transition, you may see parts of each photo until one replaces the other. Transitions can be entertaining or irritating.

- **Clock:** If the frame has a clock, you do not
  have to set the clock to use the frame.
  However, if the frame also has an option to
  turn on and off automatically at a specified
  time or to display a clock on screen, set the
  clock, including date, if that is an option.

- **Brightness and contrast:** You may be able
  to adjust the brightness and the contrast
  between light and dark. Wait until you've
  seen how your pictures look with the
  default settings.

Editing Photos for Frames

If a photo isn't exactly right, you may be able to fix it
by editing. You may be able to perform basic editing
using your camera or your frame. Your most complete
editing option is to use software on a computer, such
as the Windows Live Photo Gallery. These are the most
common editing tasks:

✓ **Rotate:** Photos taken while holding the camera
vertically, instead of horizontally, may appear
horizontally in the frame. Some cameras and
frames automatically rotate these photos.
Otherwise, you need to rotate the photos using
editing options. Many frames rotate a photo
temporarily. In such a case, the next time you
turn the frame on, the photo may be back to its
original unrotated orientation.

✓ **Crop:** By cropping a photo, you discard some of
the area around the subject to make the subject
a larger part of the photo, which is especially
good on small frames. However, if you crop a
photo, you increase the odds the frame has to

add black bars to the sides or top and bottom to fit the photo in the frame. (You can crop using the frame's aspect ratio to avoid this problem.)

Some frames enable you to zoom into a photo. This doesn't change the original photo, while letting you see part of the photo more closely. The next time you see this particular photo, it will be back to unzoomed.

✔ **Resize:** Most digital cameras produce photos that are much larger than necessary for viewing on most frames. A large photo takes more room on the memory card than a smaller photo. Large photos also take longer to copy and might display more slowly. However, you only need to resize photos if you are trying to fit more photos on the memory card for the frame. (It may be easier to buy a larger memory card.)

✔ **Adjust exposure:** A photo may be too dark or too bright. Some frames automatically adjust exposure, color, and contrast. You may be able to fix a photo's exposure.

✔ **Delete:** If a photo really is beyond saving, you can delete it using the camera's delete function or a function on the frame, if it has one. You'd be surprised what you can do to fix a photo on a computer. Consider copying all your photos from the camera to the computer, fixing them there, and putting on the frame just those photos you want to see there. See the section "Copying Photos from Your Computer."

Copying Photos from Your Computer

To copy photos from your computer to your digital frame, follow these steps:

1. **Choose a method supported by both your frame and your computer, whether a USB flash drive or a memory card.**

   If you are using a memory card, insert it into your computer's card reader. If you are using a USB flash drive, insert that into a USB port on the front or back of the computer. (If an Autoplay dialog box appears, close it.)

2. **Use Start⇨All Programs⇨Windows Live Photo Gallery.**

3. **Select the photos you intend to copy to your frame by clicking the check box in the upper left corner of each photo.**

   Your card or flash drive may hold hundreds of photos. Take advantage of tags and ratings for selecting the photos you want to display.

4. **With the mouse pointer over any one of the selected photos, click the right mouse button. Choose Copy from the context menu that appears. See Figure 3-4.**

5. Use Start⇨Computer.

The flash drive or memory card appears as a removable disk with a letter and a colon, such as E: (or whatever the last letter visible is).

6. Right-click over the icon for your flash drive or memory card. Choose Paste from the menu.

Your photos are copied to the flash drive or memory card. See Figure 3-5.

Check to select.

Number of selected photos   Choose Copy.

Figure 3-4: Copying a photo.

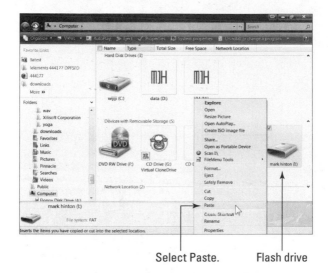

Select Paste.   Flash drive

Figure 3-5: Pasting a copy of your photo on flash drive or memory card.

7. **Remove the flash drive or memory card from your computer.**

8. **With the frame off, insert the flash drive or memory card into the appropriate slot on your frame, and turn the frame on.**

   A few seconds later, a slideshow should automatically begin to display the photos you copied.

 If your frame came with a USB cable, you can also use that to connect your frame directly to your computer. The steps are the same, except that you choose the frame in the Step 4. The frame appears as a removable disk with a letter such as E: (the last letter visible).

Chapter 4

Ten Benefits of Using Flickr

. . . .

In This Chapter

▶ Organizing your photos online

▶ Sharing your photos

▶ Getting comments on your photos

. . . .

*F*lickr (owned by Yahoo!) is a very popular photo-sharing service on the Web. You can upload your photos to Flickr to share with family, friends, and the world. This chapter highlights ten features in Flickr that help you organize and share your photos.

Although Flickr is the focus of this chapter, other comparable services are available. Each service has its strengths and weaknesses.

 Flickr does not replace photo-organizing software on your computer. You need to be able to find your photos on your own machine. Someday, you may immediately upload your pictures to the Web and never keep a local copy. Until then, organize before you upload.

Setting Up an Account Is Easy

Start by browsing www.flickr.com. If you already have a Yahoo! account, you can use that ID to log in to Flickr by following the sign in prompts. If you don't have a Yahoo! account, create a free account by following the Sign Up link on the Flickr home page.

Flickr also has Pro accounts, which cost $24.95 per year. Free accounts are limited to the 200 most recent pictures. (When you upload the 201st, the first is no longer shown to visitors, though it is still available to you.) Pro accounts are not limited in the number of pictures you can display. Pro accounts are also ad free. Free accounts have a few other relatively minor limitations.

Start with a free account. If you run into a limit you want to change, you can upgrade to a Pro account easily at any time. (You'll keep the same account information.)

After you set up an account and log in, choose You⇨Your Account and You⇨Your Profile to add more information to your account, such as your interests and location. (If you don't see the You menu item in the upper-left corner of the home screen, you need to sign in using the link in the upper-right corner.)

Uploading Photos Is a Breeze

Photostream is the term Flickr uses to describe all your photos. You add photos to your photostream by uploading them from your computer to your Flickr account.

Log in to your account on Flickr. From the menu at
the top of the screen, choose You⇨Upload Photos
and Videos. On the upload screen, browse for the
photos you want to upload. (You can also download
a free, easy-to-use tool for uploading batches of
photos.) After you select your photos, you can specify tags that will be applied to all photos that are
uploaded in one step. You can also specify what kind
of access you want to allow: public, private (only you
see them), private and visible to friends, or private
and visible to family. You identify contacts as friend
or family separately.

Figure 4-1 shows the Flash-based uploading screen.
The red arrows near the bottom of this image point
to links you can use if you want to use a forms-based
uploading tool, or if you want to download a tool and
install it on your computer.

Figure 4-1: One of Flickr's uploading screens.

Although Flickr's privacy options are good, you should realize that no security is flawless, especially when it's a service whose primary purpose is to share photos with other people. If you want absolute privacy, stay off the Web (or lurk anonymously).

You can add or change your photo's title and description anytime. Click above a photo to change its title and below to change its description. Click the Save button to save your changes or Cancel to reject a change.

Flickr reads some metadata from photos and can use that in the title and tags. Some metadata is recorded automatically by digital cameras.

Several Layouts to Choose From

Your most recently uploaded photos display first on your Flickr page, and older photos appear farther down and on other pages. This reverse chronological organization of photos is also called a *photo blog*. (Flickr also supports very short video clips.)

You can select a layout for the first page of your photostream (your Flickr home page). From the home page, follow the Change the Layout of This Page link. There are three layout options that use small images, which of course let you put more images on one page, and three layout options that use medium-sized images. Using the larger images lets you display about five photos on the home page. You can also include thumbnail links for your sets or collections.

The medium layouts show off a few pictures nicely. The small layouts show more pictures at one time. (One of the small layouts is used for all pages after your home page.)

Figure 4-2 shows a photo page with smaller thumbnails. Of the six photos in the figure, all have titles above each photo. One does not have a description below it (see the arrow). Circles indicate the You menu item, who is signed in, and views and comment count for one of the photos. Almost every item on this page — all photos and most text — can be clicked for more options or information.

Figure 4-2: Part of a Flickr photo page.

Tag Your Photos

During uploading or anytime after, you can tag photos individually or in groups. Tags provide categories for photos. Tags can be unique to you, but many tags are also used by other *Flickrers.* (Okay, we made that up. Flickr members aren't actually called *Flickrers,* but maybe they should be.) You can use tags to search for photos within your account or across all of Flickr. Your tags also create album-like groups. For example, www.flickr.com/photos/mjhinton/tags/birds/ shows all Mark's (mjhinton's) photos with *birds* as a tag, whereas www.flickr.com/photos/tags/birds/ shows everyone's photos that are tagged with birds.

To tag a photo after uploading, view the individual photo by clicking it from your photostream. Use the Add a Tag link to the right of the photo. Type a tag in the box (or multiple tags separated by spaces; tags containing spaces must be in quotation marks, such as "my friends"). You can click the link to choose from your tags if you want to use a tag you've used for another photo. To remove a tag from one photo, click the [X] next to the tag. Click a tag to see all your photos with that tag or choose You⮕Your Tags.

Figure 4-3 shows an individual photo page with the tags circled on the right. An arrow points from the Add a Tag link to the form that replaces that link when you click it.

It takes a while to get used to tagging photos, and it's fine to change your mind over time about what tags to use. The tags you add to your photos when you use Windows Photo Gallery and some other photo organizers carry over to Flickr automatically.

Figure 4-3: Tags appear on the right of individual photos.

Organize Sets and Collections

You can add photos to one or more sets during uploading or any time after. Think of a *set* as an album-like grouping. One photo can appear in any number of sets (and have any number of tags, as well). Sets display as thumbnails or larger photos with titles and descriptions. Free accounts are limited to three sets. Pro accounts can have an unlimited number of sets.

To add a photo to a set after uploading, click the Add to Set button above the photo. Click an existing set or click the link to create a new set. To remove a photo from a set, click the [X] next to the set name.

 You can give people the Web address for your Flickr photostream or the address of a specific tag or set. Browse the tag or set you want to share and copy the Web address from the address bar into an e-mail message.

Share Your Photos on Flickr

Contacts and groups make Flickr a social network through which you meet people who share an interest in photography or specific subjects. You don't have to participate in the social aspects of Flickr, but many people enjoy the interaction.

Most photos on Flickr can be viewed by anyone, including nonmembers. You can limit access to photos or the option to comment on photos to Flickr members, to your contacts, or to those contacts you identify as family or friends. You can also keep photos completely private, although that seems to defeat the purpose of a photo-sharing service.

As you explore Flickr, or as people comment on your photos, you can add other Flickr members as contacts (generally, or specifically, as friends or family). Add a contact by viewing a member's Profile (linked to his or her photo pages). Click the Add as a Contact link. (Anyone can decline the invitation to be a contact.) Your contacts appear under the Contacts menu, making it easy to keep up with new photos from contacts.

Any Flickr member can create a *group*. Groups can be open to all or restricted to invitation only. Browse a group and use the link to Join This Group. Be sure to check whether the group has specific requirements (such as that you comment on other photos). Your groups appear under the Group menu. You can contribute your photos to a group by using the Send to Group button on the photo page. To withdraw a photo from a group, click the [X] next to the group name on the right side of the individual photo page.

Add comments to other members' pictures and they'll return the favor. You can also mark any picture as a Favorite (use the star above the photo). Commenting and *favoriting* are part of the social aspect of Flickr. Activity in the form of comments and favorites raises a photo's rank and *interestingness*. (Flickr uses lots of words that vex editors.) Flickr automatically displays public photos with a high interestingness rating on its home page.

Keep Up with Recent Activity on Flickr

When you're logged in, Flickr shows how many times individual photos have been viewed, as well as sets and collections. Choose You⇨Recent Activity to see who has recently commented or marked any of your photos as favorites. Choose You⇨Stats for details on which of your photos were viewed the most yesterday or for all time, and to get a summary of counts for yesterday, this week, last week, and all time.

The Popular link on your main photostream page ranks your pictures. Photos are ranked by Interesting (calculated from all the other ranks), Views, Favorites, and Comments.

If you don't see certain menus, you may not be logged in, or missing options may be limited to Pro accounts.

Edit Your Photos in a Flash

From any single photo page, you can click the Edit link. This link opens your photo in Picnik, a Flash-based photo editor. The first time you do this, you have to authorize the connection to Picnik. You may also have to update your version of Flash — but don't worry, it's a freely available program.

Picnik provides editing tools such as Auto-fix, Rotate, Crop, and Resize. Additional options adjust exposure, colors, sharpness, and red-eye. Each of these changes has an Undo and a Redo option.

A separate Create tab adds numerous effects, text, shapes, frames, and more. When you're done editing, choose Save or cancel your changes with the Close Photo link.

Some features are available only with the premium version of Picnik, which at this writing costs $24.95 per year.

Explore the World of Flickr

Learn more about Flickr, its members, and photographic topics in general by exploring Flickr beyond your own account. From the main menu, the Explore option leads to many options. You should check out the Explore Page, Last 7 Days Interesting (yes, that's an odd phrase), and Popular Tags. That's just to start.

Go Beyond the Basics

One way to get more out of Flickr is to use your Flickr photos in a non-Flickr blog, such as Blogger or WordPress. From a single photo page, you can click the Blog This button. An alternative is to use the All Sizes button on the same screen as Blog This to obtain HTML code for the picture to paste into any Web page.

Many services connect to Flickr, with your permission, enabling you to do more with your photos than Flickr provides. This capability is based on an application program interface (API), a common mechanism for integrating Web-based services. Choose Explore➪Flickr Services to learn more.

 As you look at other people's photos and profiles, you'll discover the services they use.

Chapter 5

Ten Projects for Home and Office

* *

In This Chapter

▶ Adding your portrait to your business card

▶ Inserting photos into a word-processing document

▶ Printing a photo as a coloring-book page

▶ Capturing wide-angle views with panoramas

▶ Changing object colors with digital dye

▶ Sharing pictures in an online image gallery

▶ Replacing your screensaver with a custom slide show

▶ Using blurring techniques to produce abstract images

▶ Printing thumbnails of your image collection

▶ Creating fun and unusual photo gifts

* *

*T*hink of this chapter as one of those boxes of assorted candies, only it's serving up creative treats instead of third-rate chocolates filled with unidentifiable jellies and crèmes. The ten projects herein offer a sampling of the many ways you can incorporate digital photography into your home and work life.

Unlike a box of chocolates, this goodie tray is a no-risk proposition, too. If you bite into a project that's not to your taste, you don't need to pretend that it's delicious or hide the half-eaten candy under your napkin. Just choose the Undo command, close your image, and move on to something else.

Create a Photo Business Card

Help potential clients put a face with a name by adding your picture to your business card, as shown in Figure 5-1. You can take your finished design to any quick-print shop for reproduction on business-card paper stock.

I created the card in Figure 5-1 in Photoshop Elements, but the basic steps are the same in any photo program:

1. **Create a new image file and set the image dimensions to business-card size (2 x 3.5 inches is standard).**

Jonathan Doe Consulting

Jonathan Doe

(317) 555-1000

JDoe@ConsultMePlease.net

555 Old Town Drive   Indianapolis, IN 46200

Figure 5-1: Adding a photo to your business card makes it easier for people to remember you.

In Elements, choose File⇨New⇨Blank File. Set the Width and Height values to 2 x 3.5 inches or vice versa, depending on how you want to orient the card. Set the image resolution to 300 ppi and set the Background Contents option to white.

2. **Open your photo and crop and retouch it as needed.**

3. **Copy the photo into the new image you created in Step 1.**

   If you place the two image windows side by side, you can use the Move tool to drag the photo into the blank image.

4. **Use the tools in your photo-editing program to add the text to the card.**

It's best to create each line of text separately rather than putting it all in a single text box. Having single lines makes positioning the text elements easier.

5. **Use the Shape tools to add lines, boxes, or bullets.**

   The Shape tools share a flyout menu near the bottom of the toolbox, as shown in Figure 5-2. I used the Line tool to add the horizontal rule (line) to the business card. You simply drag with the tool to create the shape, setting the shape formatting with the controls on the options bar. (For bullets, try using the Ellipse tool.)

   In Photoshop Elements, shapes appear on their own layers and work similarly to text layers. You can find specifics in the Elements Help system.

6. **When you're finished with the card, choose File⇨Save As and save a layered version of your file.**

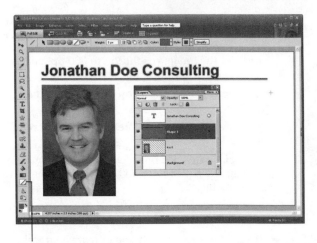

Shape tools

Figure 5-2: Use the Shape tools to create rules and bullets.

You must select either the PSD or TIFF file format and enable the Layers check box in the Save As dialog box. By retaining your individual layers, you can easily alter the text or replace the photo in the future if needed.

7. Create a single-layer version of the file to take to the copy shop for reproduction.

With the original file open, choose File➪Save As. Give the file a new name and then save it in the TIFF format with the Layers option *disabled*. This creates a flattened (single-layer) copy of the image file that you can take to your quick-print shop for reproduction. (Check with the shop first to find out about any special file-prep requirements.)

Add Pictures to a Text Document

With Photoshop Elements or another photo-editing program, you can add captions and other bits of text to an image. But the text tools found in Elements and other photo-editing programs aren't very sophisticated, so if your project calls for more than a line or two of type, you're better off creating it in a word-processing program such as Microsoft Word or Corel WordPerfect. After you enter and edit your text, you can then add a photo to the page, as I did for my professional bio, a portion of which appears in Figure 5-3.

Picture toolbar

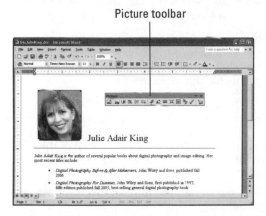

Figure 5-3: You can insert digital photos into any text document.

The following steps show you how to insert a picture into a Microsoft Word document. The basic steps for inserting pictures are the same, but — depending on the version of Word you have — the way you access the controls may vary. The figures and steps here relate to earlier versions of Word, but I added notes within the steps to point you in the right direction if you use a newer version. If you use some other word-processing program, the basic process is the same, too, but check your software's Help system for specific command names and formatting options.

1. **In your document, click the spot where you want to insert the picture.**

2. **Choose Insert⇨Picture⇨From File.**

   In Word 2007, click the Insert tab and then click the Picture icon. Either way, you then see a variation of the standard file-opening dialog box.

3. **Locate and select the picture you want to use and then click Insert.**

   Your picture appears in your document.

4. **Click the picture to select it and then choose Format⇨Picture to set the initial formatting options for the picture.**

   You see the Format Picture dialog box.

   You can skip this step in Word 2007; the Format tab should pop into view as soon as you insert your picture. (If not, click the tab.) All the options for formatting your picture appear on the tab, so you can skip Steps 5 and 6 also.

5. **Click the Layout tab and set the Wrapping Style option.**

   This setting determines *text wrapping,* which affects how the program positions your photo with respect to the text.

6. **Visit the other tabs of the dialog box to continue formatting your text and then click OK to close the dialog box.**

In addition to formatting text through the dialog box, you can click the picture to display little boxes around its perimeter, as earlier shown around the picture in Figure 5-3. Your picture is now selected and you can manipulate it as follows:

- ✔ To move the picture, click and drag it.
- ✔ To resize the photo, drag a corner handle. Remember that enlarging the photo can significantly reduce image quality.

In Word 2007, other controls for adjusting your picture appear on the Format tab. In earlier versions, you can access other controls via the Picture toolbar, labeled in Figure 5-3. To display the toolbar, choose View➪Toolbars➪Picture. For details on the toolbar controls as well as other aspects of working with graphics in Microsoft Word, check the program's Help system.

Turn a Portrait into a Coloring Book Page

Here's a fun project to do with children: Photograph your subject against a white backdrop, as shown in the left image in Figure 5-4. Then turn the photo into a coloring book page by applying a special-effects filter in your photo editor, as shown on the right.

To create the effect in Elements, follow these steps:

1. **Press D to set the foreground paint color to black.**

   The *D* stands for *default* colors — black for the foreground paint color and white for the background paint color.

2. **Choose Filter⇨Sketch⇨Photocopy.**

   The Filter Gallery dialog box appears.

Figure 5-4: You can create a personalized coloring book page by applying a special-effects filter.

3. **Adjust the sliders on the right side of the dialog box to produce an outline effect you like. Then click OK to close the dialog box.**

4. **If needed, use the Eraser tool to clean up the image.**

   When used on the Background layer, the Eraser tool applies the background paint color, which you set to white in Step 1. On the options bar, set the tool mode to Brush and the Opacity to 100% and then drag to erase any lines that you don't want in your coloring-book image.

If a large portion of the background needs help, select it by using the selection tools. Then just press Delete to make the selected area white.

5. **Establish the print size and resolution, and print the image on white paper.**

As a variation on the theme, you can create a watercolor page by printing the image on watercolor paper, assuming that you own an inkjet printer that can accept such specialty papers.

Shoot and Stitch a Panoramic Image

Can't get your entire subject to fit in the frame, even if you use your camera's widest-angle setting? Record the scene in pieces and then stitch them together in your photo editor to create a panoramic image. For example, because of the location of the house shown in Figure 5-5, I wasn't able to move far enough away to capture it all in one shot. So I shot two images, capturing different portions of the house, and then fused the images into the panoramic version shown in Figure 5-6.

Figure 5-5: Frame the segments of your panorama so that they overlap by at least 30%.

Figure 5-6: The stitched panorama appears to be a single image.

Most photo programs offer a tool that automates the process of stitching multiple photos into a panorama. In Elements, just open the photos that you want to seam and then choose File➪New➪Photomerge Panorama. You then see a dialog box that contains a preview of the stitched image, as shown in Figure 5-7. You can use the dialog box controls to tweak the stitching job if needed.

Figure 5-7: A panorama-stitcher simplifies the job of seaming multiple images.

For the most part, automated panorama stitching pro-grams work very well and are easy to use *if* — and this is a big *if* — you shoot your original pictures cor-rectly. Follow these guidelines:

- ✔ **Maintain the correct axis of rotation as you pan the camera.**
- ✔ **Keep the camera on the same level for each shot.**
- ✔ **Maintain the same focus distance, aperture, and exposure for each frame.**
- ✔ **Overlap each shot by at least 30 percent.** For example, in my panorama, both original images include the front porch area and a portion of the garage. This overlap gives the stitching program reference points that it needs to assemble the images correctly.
- ✔ **Watch out for people moving through the scene.**

If you follow these guidelines, your stitching program should be able to produce a seamless composite with very little trouble. Because each program works a little differently, check your software's Help system or user manual to find out exactly how to use the stitching function if you don't work with Elements.

Change the Color of an Object

Suppose that you have a product shot that features, say, a blue background, like the one on the right in Figure 5-8. But then for some reason, you need a dif-ferently colored background — perhaps the image is going on a Web page, and your original background clashes with the page background, or you just decide on another color scheme for aesthetic reasons.

Figure 5-8: To change the background, I selected it and filled it with a new color in my photo-editing program.

You can make this change easily in most photo editors. Here's the most efficient way:

1. **Use the Photoshop Elements (or your program's) selection tools to select the area of the photo that you want to change.**

2. **Open the Layers palette (Window⇨Layers) and create a new, empty layer.**

   Just click the New Layer icon, shown in Figure 5-9.

3. **Select Color from the Layer palette's Blending Mode control, labeled in Figure 5-9.**

4. **Fill the selected area with paint.**

   The quickest way to fill the selection with your new color is to choose Edit⇨Fill Selection, which opens the Fill Layer dialog box. Inside the dialog box, choose Color from the drop-down list to open the Color Picker and select your paint color. Click OK to close the Color Picker and click OK again to close the Fill Layer dialog box.

Figure 5-9: The Color blending mode is the secret to realistic color changes.

Keep in mind that after you paint, you can adjust the opacity of the paint if needed by using the Opacity control in the Layers palette. And you can easily experiment with other paint colors by using the Hue/Saturation filter.

5. **Merge the paint layer with the underlying image by choosing Layer➪Flatten Image.**

Unfortunately, when you use the Color blending mode, pixels that are completely white or black don't change. If you need to recolor black or white pixels, follow the same steps but set the Blending Mode control to Normal. Then lower the layer opacity (by using the Opacity control in the Layers palette) as needed to produce the results you want.

Create a Web Photo Gallery

Have a bunch of photos that you'd like to share online with friends and family? Don't waste your time (and that of your recipients) by attaching the images one by one to an e-mail message. Instead, create an online gallery of your photos.

You can create and post a gallery in several ways:

- ✔ Join a free online photo-sharing site such as Kodak Gallery (www.kodakgallery.com) or Snapfish (www.snapfish.com). You use the site's software to upload your images and arrange them into albums. Then you can send e-mail invites to everyone you want to be able to view the photos. Visitors can order prints of their favorite images — saving you the time and expense of doing so.

  Note that most sites that provide free photo sharing require that you buy a print or some other photo product during the year. If you don't, your pictures are usually deleted.

- ✔ Purchase a membership in an album site such as Phanfare, at www.phanfare.com. (A one-year membership to Phanfare is currently about $50.) The advantage to a paid site is that you usually get more storage space for your pictures, which means that you can upload full-resolution pictures to your gallery, an option not available on all free sites. If you need a convenient way to get high-resolution photos to clients or colleagues, this type of site is a great option. Paid sites also aren't cluttered with the advertising common on free sites.

- ✔ If you have your own Web site or have access to free pages via your Internet provider, you can create your own custom image gallery. Most photo-editing programs offer templates for creating galleries. For example, in Photoshop Elements, you would choose File⇨Create⇨ Photo Galleries.

Create a Slide-Show Screen Saver

When your computer is turned on but not in use, the monitor probably displays a *screen saver,* a series of graphics or images that move across the screen. You can replace the prefab screen savers that ship with the Windows and Mac operating systems with one that features your favorite images. The next two sections give you the steps.

Putting together a screen saver in Windows 7

To create a screen saver in Windows 7, take these steps:

1. **Put the images that you want to feature in the screensaver in a separate folder.**

   If you don't want to move the pictures out of their current folders for organizational purposes, just make copies to use for the slide show. Then put the copies in a new folder.

   To really do the job correctly, you should resize all the photos to the resolution of your monitor. Okay, so you don't absolutely *have* to — Windows will adjust the size of the pictures on the fly in the screensaver — but you didn't hear it from me.

2. **Right-click an empty area of the Windows desktop and choose Personalize from the pop-up menu that appears.**

3. **In the Personalization window, click the Screen Saver option near the bottom right.**

The Screen Saver settings dialog box appears, as shown in Figure 5-10.

Figure 5-10: Use the Windows slideshow feature to create a custom screen saver.

4. **Click the Screen Saver drop-down list and select the Photos option.**

You see what the screen saver will look like in the top half of the dialog box.

5. **With the Photos option selected, click the Settings button**

The Photos Screen Saver Settings dialog box appears, as shown in Figure 15-11.

6. **Click the Browse button and find the folder that contains the photos you planned to use for the screen saver slide show.**

7. **Select the slide show speed from the drop-down list and select the Shuffle Pictures check box if you want the pictures to display randomly.**

8. **Click Save to save your settings and return to the Screen Saver Settings dialog box.**

Figure 5-11: Specify the folder that contains the images you want to include in the slide show.

9. **Select the Wait time and password option as desired and then click Apply.**

If you enable the password control, be sure to write down your password or choose one that's easy to remember! If you forget the password, you won't be able to stop the screen saver to access your normal computer functions.

Creating a photo screen saver on a Mac

If you use a Macintosh computer, follow these steps to create a slide-show screen saver:

1. **Open the System Preferences dialog box by choosing System Preferences from the Apple menu.**

2. **Click the Show All icon and then click the Desktop and Screen Saver icon to display the dialog box shown in Figure 5-12.**

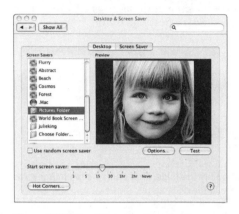

Figure 5-12: On a Mac, create your screen saver via the Desktop and Screen Saver panel of the System Preferences dialog box.

3. **Click the Screen Saver button to display the options you see in Figure 5-12.**

4. **From the Screen Savers list on the left side of the dialog box, choose the folder that contains the images that you want to include in the screen saver.**

   If the folder you want isn't visible, click the Choose Folder option to access additional folders on your system. Click Choose after you find the folder you want to return to the dialog box shown in Figure 5-12.

5. **Use the other controls in the dialog box to customize the screen saver timing and display.**

Blur Your Way to an Abstract Image

Want to give a collage or other photo composition an interesting background? You can play around with special effects filters or fill your canvas with prefab patterns or textures, but here's another idea: First, find a colorful object to photograph. Then, when you take the picture, simply move your camera slightly back and forth during the exposure. The result will be a blurry pattern featuring the colors in the subject.

To achieve a significant blur, you need a slow shutter speed. If your camera doesn't offer manual exposure or shutter-priority exposure — meaning you have no direct control over shutter speed — try using Nighttime scene mode, if that's available, or check your camera manual to discover other scene modes that may produce a slower shutter.

Of course, if you can't produce the extent of blur you like in camera, you can increase the blur in your photo editor. For example, Elements has additional blur options. Just experiment until you get the look you like.

Print a Contact Sheet

A *contact sheet,* in photography lingo, is simply a page that contains thumbnails of a batch of images. You can print a contact sheet that shows thumbnails of all the photos that you copied onto a CD or DVD, for example. I take this step every time I archive my images onto a CD, in fact, so that when I'm searching for an image, I can just scan my contact sheets instead of loading CDs into my CD drive.

Most photo-organizer programs offer a command that prints contact sheets. In the Elements 5.0 Organizer, for example, you select the folder or images that you want to include on the contact sheet and then choose File⇨Print. In the resulting dialog box, shown in Figure 5-13, select Contact Sheet from the Select Type of Print drop-down list, as shown in the figure. You can then specify various aspects of the contact sheet, including the number of thumbnails per page and what data prints with each thumbnail. The center of the dialog box shows a preview of the contact sheet.

Figure 5-13: You can print a contact sheet showing thumbnails of selected images.

If you use iPhoto, the free organizer provided with recent versions of the Mac operating system, you create a contact sheet in much the same way. Select the images to include on the sheet, click the Print button, and then select Contact Sheet from the Style drop-down list in the resulting dialog box.

Creating One-of-a-Kind Photo Gifts

You probably already know that you can use your digital photos to create custom greeting cards, calendars, and other standard print products. Most photo programs offer templates that simplify the process, and, if you're short on time or energy, just about any quick-print shop, online print service, or local photo lab can do the job for you.

You may not be aware, though, of some of the more unusual types of gifts that you can create from your photos. Here are some of my favorites:

- ✔ **Photo postage stamps:** That's right, you don't have to be famous and dead to get your picture on a postage stamp. One online company offering this product is PhotoStamps (http://photo.stamps.com). Some digital-print kiosks found in photo labs also enable you to produce your own stamps. And, yes, the stamps are accepted as standard postage by the post office.

- ✔ **Notebook skins:** A *notebook skin* is a self-sticking vinyl cover that you can adhere to your laptop computer case — think grade-school book jacket done up for the digital age. Companies such as Skinit (www.skinit.com) enable you to upload a favorite photo and turn it into your own, personal notebook skin. You can also create skins for mobile phones, MP3 players, and other digital devices.

- ✔ **Pillows and other home décor items:** By printing your images on fabric transfer paper, available for most inkjet printers, you can create pillows, blankets, baby bibs, and any other type of fabric-based gift or decorator item you can imagine.

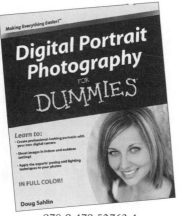

After you've read the Portable Edition, look for the original *For
Dummies* book on the topic. The handy Contents at a Glance below
highlights the information you'll get when you purchase a copy of
Digital Photography For Dummies, 6th Edition — available wherever
books are sold, or visit Dummies.com.

Contents at a Glance